THE ESSENTIAL GUIDE TO

mold making & slip casting

andrew martin

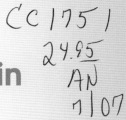

LARK BOOKS
A Division of Sterling Publishing Co., Inc.
New York

editors
Chris Rich, Suzanne J. E. Tourtillott

art director
Megan Kirby

cover designer
Barbara Zaretsky

assistant editor
Shannon P. Quinn-Tucker

associate art director
Shannon Yokeley

art production assistant
Jeff Hamilton

editorial assistance
Delores Gosnell

art interns
Courtney Tiberio, Amelia Hancock

illustrator
Olivier Rollin

photographer
Nick Elias

I dedicate this book to my Heart-Master, Adi Da Samraj, who has shown me that self-transcendence is the essence and the purpose of both life and making art.

Library of Congress Cataloging-in-Publication Data

Martin, Andrew (Andrew J.)

  The essential guide to mold making & slip casting / Andrew Martin. -- 1st ed.

    p. cm.

  Includes index.

  ISBN 1-60059-077-2 (hardcover)

  1. Pottery craft. 2. Pottery molds. 3. Slips (Ceramics) 4. Slip casting. I. Title.

  TT920.M3653 2007

  738.1'42--dc22

10 9 8 7 6 5 4 3 2 1

First Edition

Published by Lark Books, A Division of Sterling Publishing Co., Inc.
387 Park Avenue South, New York, N.Y. 10016

Previously published as *The Definitive Guide to Mold Making and Slip Casting*
Published by MAGUS Art Publications & Workshops
369-B Third St., Suite 105, San Rafael, CA 94901

Text © 2006, Andrew Martin
Photography © 2006, Lark Books
Illustrations © 2006, Lark Books
Special photography: Suzanne J. E. Tourtillott, page 9

Distributed in Canada by Sterling Publishing,
c/o Canadian Manda Group, 165 Dufferin Street
Toronto, Ontario, Canada M6K 3H6

Distributed in the United Kingdom by GMC Distribution Services,
Castle Place, 166 High Street, Lewes, East Sussex, England BN7 1XU

Distributed in Australia by Capricorn Link (Australia) Pty Ltd.,
P.O. Box 704, Windsor, NSW 2756 Australia

If you have questions or comments about this book, please contact:
Lark Books
67 Broadway
Asheville, NC 28801
(828) 253-0467

Manufactured in China

ISBN 13: 978-1-60059-077-1
ISBN 10: 1-60059-077-2

For information about custom editions, special sales, premium and corporate purchases, please contact Sterling Special Sales Department at 800-805-5489 or specialsales@sterling-pub.com.

contents

introduction

I first encountered slip casting in 1978, as an undergraduate student at the Kansas City Art Institute. In response to a class assignment in nonthrown forms, I figured out how to make a mold for a tray by pouring plaster over a slab of clay. Smitten by the mold-making process but utterly ignorant, I fumbled through my earliest slip-casting attempts, using slip blended up right out of the stoneware slop bucket. The results were less than magnificent. Despite these obstacles, I persevered. I had recognized right away that slip casting allows a potter to explore non-round forms; the forms to which I was attracted were nonconcentric and therefore had to be made with molds. The process was loaded with possibilities that appealed to my aesthetic, technical, mechanical, and conceptual predilections.

I would later learn that the development of plaster molds and slip casting in Europe revolutionized the ceramic industry of the eighteenth and nineteenth centuries by allowing mass production of highly refined, often elaborately ornate forms. These developments—and the inexpensive industrial wares that they made possible—wiped out the economy of local cottage-industry potters. The 1920s, however, brought about the birth of the studio pottery movement, one that can be attributed to Bernard Leach, an Asian-

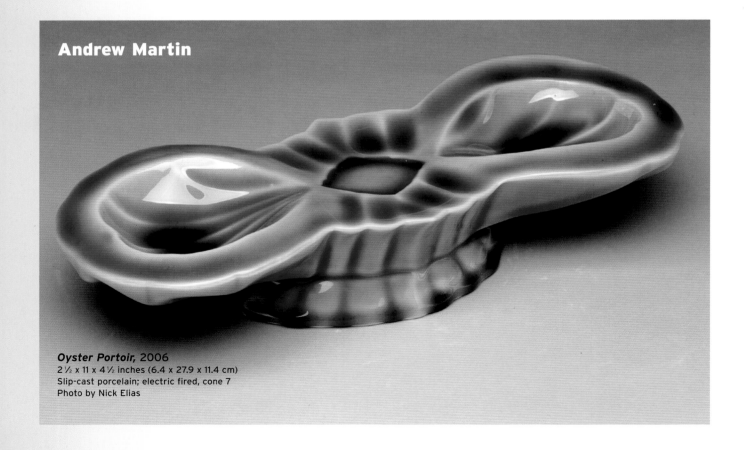

Andrew Martin

Oyster Portoir, 2006
2 ½ x 11 x 4 ½ inches (6.4 x 27.9 x 11.4 cm)
Slip-cast porcelain; electric fired, cone 7
Photo by Nick Elias

Andrew Martin

Slumping Gourds, 1990
13 ½ x 6 x 6 inches (34.3 x 15.2 x 15.2 cm)
Slip-cast porcelain; wood fired, cone 13
Photo by Nick Elias

born Englishman, who passionately promoted the philosophy and beauty of handmade functional pottery.

Because Leach disliked mold-made industrial wares, he eschewed molds entirely; he thought they destroyed the individuality of pots and potters. Leach's antimold sentiments were actually anti-industrial, yet they influenced the ceramic art field for decades, and this prejudice was still in effect when I began using molds as a student. I was in both camps: my interest was in making pottery, and I was compelled by pottery forms that could be made only with molds.

Artists of my generation have rediscovered the unique challenges and rewards of slip casting. Today, as in older cultures, molds aren't viewed philosophically, but as tools like any others. The artist who uses them must have an aesthetic vision. If the work is about the tool, the tool will determine the result. Slip casting, used as a means to an aesthetic end, is the approach that came into play quite naturally and is finally enjoying a renaissance among studio potters. Creative ceramic artists are slip casting everything from elegant tableware lines and one-of-a-kind, highly decorated series of forms to technically awe-inspiring sculptural assemblages.

While I was at Alfred University, I chose slip casting and mold making as the exclusive focus of my working process. I was inevitably faced with solving technical challenges that weren't being taught in classes. Published texts on slip casting were few and far between at that time; most of my earliest education came in the form of oral histories from my teachers. The industrial techniques that comprised much of what was being taught didn't resonate with my own aesthetics. By the time I reached graduate school at Alfred University, I had realized that I wanted to make slip-cast tableware and pots that embraced

Andrew Martin

Papillion Coffer, 2006
Slip-cast porcelain; electric fired, cone 7
6 x 17 x 5 (15.2 x 43.2 x 12.7 cm)
Photo by Nick Elias

every kind of complexity in their visual language. Feet, spouts, lids, handles—I wanted to make them all with molds. And as an added challenge, I decided to make brushwork decoration part of each form.

My first major challenge was how to make lids. None of the methods I had learned were fast, easy, or exact. Ceramic engineers could tell me how to slip cast a round lid, but these lids didn't fit well. I wanted all my lids to fit perfectly: inset lids, cap lids, every style of lid. Thus, my goal—to produce complex, highly crafted slipware—necessarily led me to create many of the techniques found in this book.

By the time I left graduate school, I had adopted the basic techniques that became the foundation for my own approach to slip casting, including the unique template system that I now use to design pots. This system allows me to draw a two-dimensional line and, by copying that line to a template that becomes part of the prototype for

the pot, to carry the line into three-dimensional space. The aesthetic, technical, and design challenges I faced as I developed this template system were all linked—and solved—together. Designing a lid that fit perfectly, no matter the shape, was my first major breakthrough. Methods for making footwells in saucers, adding hollow-cast feet to support heavy vases, and the development of more complex molds followed.

After Alfred and before I opened my studio, I worked in the reproductions department at the Metropolitan Museum of Art in New York. Every evening after hours, I would stroll through the Islamic and Chinese collections, visiting my favorite pots and slowly unraveling the aesthetic and technological mysteries of hundreds of years past. Here were the works of some of the first experts to demonstrate that creative technical invention could lead to great pots. The Chinese wing of the museum featured delicately beautiful Ding-ware bowls, shaped on hump

molds and with thrown feet. One of my favorite Islamic vases had a thrown-bowl base, a molded bowl with floral carving for the shoulder, and a thrown neck. Even the Moche potters of Peru used molds to make their famous portrait heads with molded stirrup handles.

Industrial slip-casting techniques haven't been of much assistance to me over the years. Industry emphasizes the use of plaster prototypes; too often, these plaster models result in pots that look like plaster and that feel mechanical and minimalist. I've always been much more interested in pots that look as if they were hand-made, so I've usually relied on clay prototypes instead.

Twenty thousand pots later, after spending three decades in the studio developing my own techniques through trial and error, teaching dozens of workshops, and having countless conversations with fellow potters, I decided to distill what I had learned by writing a book. I made the decision to do so one evening after teaching the first day of a workshop in Vermont. I was telling a friend how impossible it felt to explain everything in a two-day workshop, and added that I was considering writing a book. Her response was immediate: "Of course you should write a book!"

The result was a self-published book that I also distributed. In 2006 Lark Books invited me to update and revise that initial publication. You're now holding the much better version—*The Essential Guide to Mold Making and Slip Casting*, which includes new technical data, new recipes, full-color how-to photographs to help the reader make each project, and a wonderful photo gallery of works by some of today's finest artists.

The Essential Guide to Mold Making and Slip Casting is designed to make the subject of mold making accessible to a wide range of artists, from beginners to experts, and from ceramists to artists who work with other materials. Because its focus is fundamentally on molding and casting forms, not just on making and using molds for clay slip, some of the techniques I describe can be applied to casting sculpture, tile, concrete, and glass, as well as to press-molding clay.

Within these pages beginners will find a complete introduction to the art and science of designing and making molds, and using them to cast pieces from simple plates to complex teapots. The heart of this book is devoted to detailed instructions for making molds of one or more pieces, as well as plaster and rubber master molds. Instructions for designing the prototypes from which molds are cast, using my template system, mixing and pouring plaster, formulating slip, and casting the molds you make are all included, as are descriptions of basic tools and materials, my favorite slip recipes, and a troubleshooting section to help you solve problems that you may encounter.

You'll also find profiles of five artists whom I consider to be exceptional in today's slip-casting arena. One of the most exciting developments in this arena is the range of both aesthetic and technical skills that these artists demonstrate. Unfortunately, one of the featured artists, Anne Kraus, who was a friend of mine in graduate school, has passed away. Her delightful pots are markers, as they were when she was alive, that illustrate her journey of self-discovery and feeling in both objective and subjective worlds.

I love the fluidity of clay and glaze and fire, and have imagined my pots as filled with the sense of joy, generosity, and fluidity that clay offers. By sheer necessity, the systems that I've developed in order to meet my goals have been tested and refined many times over. Yet the evolution of my work always demands new solutions to new problems. While *The Essential Guide to Mold Making and Slip Casting* contains many of the solutions I've found, your challenge and opportunity are to invent your own.

As you'll soon discover, slip casting is both a body of techniques and a world of aesthetics. I've always worked as a potter and have therefore fit the slip-casting process to my view of how pots should look, feel, and work. When I teach workshops, I'm always delighted by how the participants adapt these techniques to their own points of view. As you try these techniques yourself, don't be overly concerned about doing things "right" the first time. Just jump right in, as I did. Take what you can use and invent what you need.

Happy slip casting!

Andrew Martin

Tamba Tums, 2000
5½ x 3 x 3 inches (13 x 7.6 x 7.6 cm)
Slip-cast porcelain; wood fired, cone 12
Photo by Nick Elias

an overview

an overview

I approach mold making as an integral part of the creative process, not just as a tool. For example, before making molds for slip casting, you must create a full-scale prototype of the form you wish to cast. Some artists visualize what they want to make and then use the technology to create it. Others simply start working with materials and techniques, and intuitively feel their way to the finished forms. And some artists do some of both. My approach allows for both methods. In fact, while exploring these systems, you may discover a whole new way of looking at how to make a pottery form.

Here's a secret about mold making that most experts don't teach: very few rules can't be broken. In my 30 years of trial and error, one thing I've definitely learned is that there is more than one way to do almost everything. Although the techniques in this book have evolved from my years of experience, at some point you'll need to go beyond my "rules." Take what is useful and invent what you need.

The artistic process necessitates going beyond any knowledge you're given; you must add your own voice to the discussion. I developed my own skills by going beyond what I learned from others, and even by going beyond my own presumed limits and ideas about myself. Transcending myself in the midst of the artistic process is the key to manifesting art that I never even would have imagined making. Somehow, when "I" get out of the way, something greater kicks in!

At its most basic level, *slip casting* is the process of pouring a liquid clay mixture called *casting slip* into a plaster mold in order to shape a clay object, known as a *casting*. The mold absorbs water from the casting slip, which dries and stiffens around the walls of the mold. Most slip-casting molds are created by pouring plaster over a *prototype*—a form *modeled* from clay or plaster, or a found object. Some potters use slip-casting techniques to increase production by creating many identical pieces; other ceramists use molds to make one-of-a-kind forms that can't be shaped by any other process.

Many materials suggest interesting forms for prototypes.

DESIGNING & MAKING PROTOTYPES

Among all the varieties of pottery forms to make, the following are just a few possibilities: dinnerware, tableware, teapots, cookware, vases, candlesticks, and pitchers. Each of these can suggest a dozen or more possible forms. Where should you start? Read through this book to find a pottery form that appeals to you or a method of making prototypes that suits your ability, aesthetic, and spirit of adventure.

selecting materials for prototypes

Begin by either choosing materials that fit your existing idea for a prototype or playing with different materials to come up with an idea (see photo 1).

Clay, plaster, wood, polystyrene foam, plants, stones, shells, steel plates, toys, and duct tape—you can make a prototype from almost any material or materials, in almost any combination. It's easy to fall in love with using found objects as prototypes; just don't forget to be an artist! Ask yourself if there's a particular portion of that object that appeals to you, and whether you'd like to adapt it. If you do use found objects or preexisting forms, the key is knowing how you'd like to interpret them.

making clay prototypes

My basic systems for making prototypes include the use of clay, hardboard *templates* (rigid sheets on which clay is modeled to create the prototype), and plaster. No matter which materials or system you use, your prototype may require a one-piece or multiple-piece mold. The goal is to make a mold that consists of as few pieces as necessary. If you want cast pieces that are very organic and easy to make, use clay for your prototype. For more well-defined shapes, I've developed a template system in which I combine clay with shapes cut from hardboard.

Clay is the most forgiving material for modeling prototypes that are easy to mold and slip cast. I also prefer clay prototypes because the resulting pottery actually looks like clay. Finished pots made from plaster *models* (or prototypes) that have been turned on a wheel or lathe often end up looking like plaster.

From clay prototypes, you can make simple one-piece molded plates, tumblers, and serving dishes. You can also use solid clay prototypes for two-piece molded pitchers, vases, and planters. And if you want a challenge, try a complex clay prototype, such as my teapot, which requires a six-piece mold (see pages 101–105).

Lauren Adams

Tumblers, 2005
5 x 3 x 3 inches (12.7 x 7.6 x 7.6 cm)
Cast porcelain from thrown form; inlaid copper carbonate; oxidation fired, cone 6
Photo by Robert Puglisi

David Pier

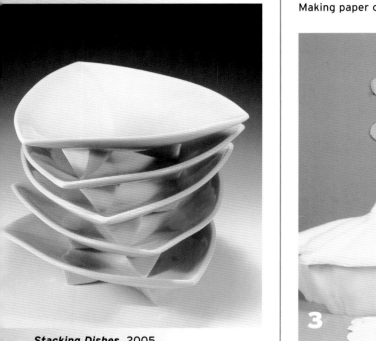

Stacking Dishes, 2005
8 x 8 x 8 inches (20.3 x 20.3 x 20.3 cm)
Porcelain slip; electric fired, cone 10, oxidation
Photo by artist

Making paper cutouts of profiles

Making paper cutouts of shapes

designing prototypes with templates

By using the template system described in this book, you can make very elaborate prototypes for complex molds, as well as simpler prototypes for one-piece molds.

In graduate school, when I was still modeling all my clay prototypes

directly on the table, I had a problem with the platters I was making. Because their *pitch* (the degree of a steep downward curve) was carried all the way to the tops of the rims, they always had feather-thin edges. My attempts to give the rims verticality, for more visual and structural strength, were only intermittently successful. Then one day it occurred to me that I

4

Cutting a template for a prototype

templates, and later I developed a template system to make feet that matched the bodies of forms exactly.

Now I generate most of the shapes of my forms by first drawing *profiles* (side views of a form) and *shapes* (top views) on paper and cutting them out (see photos 2 and 3). Then I transfer the cutouts to hardboard, from which I cut templates that I incorporate right into my prototypes (see photo 4). Templates, which can be made for the shape of a pot, for its profile, or for both, provide a way to move designs from two dimensions to three dimensions.

making plaster prototypes

Although plaster is my least favorite prototype material, I do use it in some instances. For example, I use blocks of plaster to carve one-piece molds for shot glasses and tumblers (see page 54). Sometimes I use leftover batches of liquid plaster to model prototypes—an exercise in timing because the plaster sets as you work. I also use chunks of plaster to model three-dimensional prototype "sketches." As with other materials, you can use plaster prototypes to make very complex molds, as well as one-piece molds.

could use hardboard templates to produce prototypes; hardboard is very easy to cut with a jigsaw. The templates added both visual and technical strength to the rims of my plates. Soon after I figured out several ways to make perfectly fitted lids by using

Another approach to making prototypes is to create a collage with chunks and slabs of dried plaster. You can nail the plaster pieces together because plaster, like wood, is filled with air, so it won't break; the nails just displace air. After you've assembled the plaster pieces, test them to see if they move at all. If they do, use epoxy or wood glue to add strength to the nailed areas. Then fill in the spaces with plastic clay.

calculating slip shrinkage

I like to use asparagus, strawberries, and other fruits and vegetables as prototype materials. When I do, however, I have to procure unusually large samples because my slip shrinks by 12 percent during firing. Taking shrinkage into account is even more critical in slip casting than in throwing; when you throw, you can adjust pot sizes as you go along. Remember, investing your energy in the mold-making process can save you time by allowing you to reproduce pots relatively quickly, but you'll waste time if you don't create the right size prototype at the very beginning.

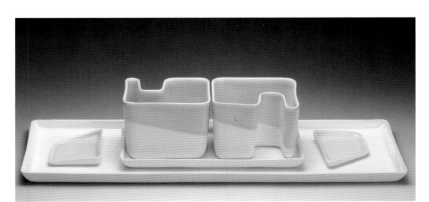

Heather Mae Erickson

Finnspired, 2005
3 ¼ x 17 ½ x 6 inches (8.3 x 44.5 x 15.2 cm)
Plaster models, stoneware slip; oxidation fired,
white glaze, cone 6; blue glaze, cone 8
Photo by Ken Yanoviak

To help you calculate the correct size for your prototype, use the following example and algebraic equation:

Let's say you're using my slip recipe (see page 151), which shrinks 12 percent (just insert a different percentage for whatever slip you're using), and you're planning to make a tile that will be 10 inches (25.4 cm) square after firing. Subtract the shrinkage percentage from 100 to get the percentage size for the fired tile. In this example, the fired tile will be 88 percent as large as the original tile.

Now you can use the following equation, where x represents the size of your prototype:

$$\frac{\text{Desired size of finished piece}}{x} = \frac{\text{\% of original after firing}}{100}$$

Or, in our example:

$$\frac{10 \text{ inches (25.4 cm)}}{x} = \frac{88}{100}$$

Cross-multiply the numbers to get the following:

$$88x = 1000$$

Divide 1000 by 88 to solve x. In this case, $x = 11.4$.

Therefore, to make a finished tile that is 10 inches (25.4 cm) square, the prototype must be 11.4 inches—or approximately 11⅜ inches (29 cm) square.

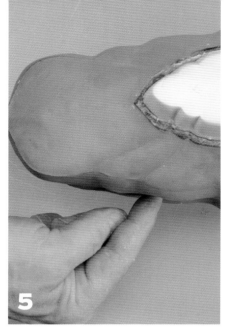

5

Checking for an undercut

6

Evaluating a form for a two-piece mold

DESIGNING, MAKING & USING MOLDS

Beginners often make or use forms with *undercuts*—indented or undulating areas in a form that cause it to lock (or stick) inside the mold. Undercuts offer valuable experience; solving the problems they cause will teach you a lot! I wouldn't recommend going out of your way to try making a mold with undercuts.

Checking your prototype for even the smallest of undercuts before designing your mold is essential. One way to do this is to run your fingertip down the form while you look at it from directly above. If at any point on the form, you can't see your fingertip, you've located an undercut (see photo 5). In addition, you can often feel an undercut, even if you can't see it.

Mold making is like map making. If, with your prototype upside down on the work surface, you can see its entire exterior from directly above, you can make the mold in one piece. If you can't see the whole exterior, the proto-

type has one or more undercuts. Look at the prototype from one side and then from the other. Can you see the whole form from these two angles? If you can, you can make a two-piece mold from the prototype (see photo 6). One mold section will form the floor and half of the exterior wall, and the second section will form the remainder (see page 66). If you can't see the whole exterior of the prototype from two vantage points, the form will require a mold of at least three pieces. The form always determines the piece count.

You'll probably need to study complex forms before you fully understand the mechanics of designing multiple-piece molds. Even a cup might require a three-piece mold. In the meantime, here are a couple of tips. First, when you look at one side of a form, the edges are a good place to split the mold design; splitting the mold at the edges makes it easy to clean the seams from the casting. (The areas where mold sections meet leave seam marks, traditionally known as *fettles,* on the cast piece.) And second, in multiple-piece molds, the last mold section to be made is the first to be removed after casting. The goal is to release stress from the casting as it shrinks and dries so that it doesn't crack where it's indented. Visualize the sequence in which the mold will be made, the sequence in which you'll disassemble and reassemble it, and how it will release the casting. Don't be concerned if these processes aren't immediately obvious to you; you'll acquire visualization skills after making a few molds.

keeping molds simple

Beginning mold makers tend to go overboard and make very well designed but overly complex molds. You'll discover over time that molds can usually be made with fewer pieces than you might have believed. At each step in the process, I try to eliminate any unnecessary, time-consuming steps without compromising my aesthetic standards. The process is about making ceramics with plaster molds—not about obsessing over plaster itself.

drain-cast & solid-cast molds

Drain-cast molds are used to create hollow castings, and range from simple one-piece molds, such as those for bowls, to complex molds for casting teapots. First, slip is poured into the mold and allowed to sit while the plaster mold absorbs water from it. The slip around the mold's interior surfaces begins to thicken and harden to form what will be the finished piece (or casting). As soon as the desired casting thickness is achieved, the excess slip is poured out of the mold. Most of the molds I use are drain cast.

Solid-cast molds are more specialized. Slip is poured into them and is left in place, rather than drained out, until the cast piece becomes solid. These molds are often used to cast tiles and small handles.

considering weight

Technical and practical considerations should determine the thickness of your molds. The main reason to keep molds on the thin side is that thin molds are easier to move during the casting process. Lighter molds can help to save your spine! For durability's sake, I tend to make my molds on the thicker side, from a minimum of 1½ inches (3.8 cm) up to 2 inches (5.1 cm) thick, although some have parts that are more than 3 inches (7.6 cm) thick. I make thicker molds for forms such as tumblers so that I can cast them up to six or seven times in one day. Molds that are cast this often will become so saturated with water that they won't absorb quickly, and the castings won't release from them. Any molds that you use this heavily should be dried overnight for the next day's casting. Most molds aren't likely to become saturated, even if you cast them a few times in one day.

Making large forms is a physical and technical challenge, but the methods for creating them are no different from those used to make the other molds covered in this book. Just design the form and mold so that casting, draining, and removing cast pieces can be executed with as little lifting as possible.

The logistics can be formidable if a mold holds more than 5 gallons (18.9 L) of casting slip. In molds that split vertically, the pressure exerted by

Chris Gustin

Alcobaca Vase #0313, 2003
25 x 9 x 8 inches (63.5 x 22.9 x 20.3 cm)
Slip-cast porcelain; wood fired in anagama kiln, cone 11
Photo by Dean Powell

7

Notice the slumping in this plate.

the liquid slip will try to push the mold sections apart. This moment will be one of sheer frustration and will provide an elemental lesson in physics. The most important step to take when casting any multiple-piece mold is to band the sections together tightly. Doing this is even more important with very large or tall molds that have vertical seams. Use self-tensioning belts, available at ceramic suppliers. If you don't have these types of belts on hand, for extra security add wooden wedges under the belts that you do have.

I embed a drain in the bottom of each of my largest molds so that I don't have to lift the molds when I drain them. Parts used for drip-feed irrigation work very well for this purpose. I use a tube with a screw-on cap and a short piece of tubing that slips into it. To drain the slip, I simply unscrew the cap and let the slip drain into a bucket. Then I tilt the mold so that the remaining slip in the bottom flows to the drain. Mold disassembly is usually executed while the mold remains in a standing position.

Sometimes I make a mold too thick in order to make it more quickly,

and then cut off the excess plaster with a bow saw. Remove the saw marks with a *Surform tool* and *wet/dry sandpaper*. (Surform tools are similar to rasps; wet/dry sandpaper is a silicon carbide paper that won't dissolve on wet surfaces.)

Some potters may want to switch to slip casting because it doesn't require the repetitive motions of bending over a potter's wheel or wedging clay. If your back and wrists are shot from throwing, slip casting can offer a new range of motion for your body, but it still requires a lot of heavy lifting. I maintain a regular routine of calisthenics and yoga to strengthen my back and stay in good condition.

taking slip slumping into account

Thrown clay forms are less likely to *slump* (become deformed) because they're aided both by the compression caused by throwing and the ceramist's ability to leave some areas thicker for support. Slip casting, however, is a process of sedimentation, so cast forms are of equal thickness throughout and are not compressed. A cast form must have enough structure to withstand the firing, during which time the clay becomes very soft. Slumping usually occurs with very flat or cantilevered forms.

Lids tend to slump and warp if they're too flat. They'll slump less if you add

Larry J. Donahue

□'s & ○'s *Tessellated Cups*, 2006
6 ¾ x 5 x 3 ½ inches (17.1 x 12.7 x 8.9 cm)
Slip-cast porcelain; reduction fired; underglaze, trailed drawings
Photo by Christopher L. Donahue

slightly more arch to the curve than might look normal. If a cast, fired lid does slump, you can add more arch to the mold by sanding it with wet/dry sandpaper under running water. Even if the adjustment you make is slight, it will usually eliminate the slumping problem. (At Kohler Co., the well-known plumbing manufacturer and home of the John Michael Kohler Arts Center, toilet-tank lids are made in just this way. The mold for the lid has a slight arch, and when the cast lid is fired, it slumps to nearly flat.)

Lids are fired on top of the bodies they fit. If the incline of the body as it rises from the foot is severe, the weight of a lid may cause the body beneath it to slump during firing. All forms are different, and the best thing to do is experiment with them. Knowledge and information offer a measure of safety, but your forms must work in practice, too.

Plates that are too flat may also tend to slump (see photo 7). When the form is indented, this type of warping tends to encourage cracking, as well. Forms that are long, straight, and cantilevered, such as elongated plates, may warp, too, because the clay isn't compressed and can't be thickened to add support to the pitch. (Visualize a long piece of stiff paper. When it's standing on edge, it will stay straight, but if you hold it at a 45-degree angle, it sags.) Smaller forms, such as saucers, aren't as susceptible to serious warping and can be cast quite flat.

I've come to accept some slumping in many cases. Slip-cast *porcelain* (a white, high-fire clay body) inevitably slumps, for example. All of my plates warp a little, but if my castings are all the same thickness, every plate warps exactly the

same way. Depending on your aesthetic, slumping may not be a problem. Casting thicker can also decrease or eliminate slumping, but preventing slumping entirely is a bit like trying to keep water from running downhill.

pouring or frosting a plaster mold

The basic steps to making a one-piece mold by pouring plaster over it are quite simple. First, you assemble a plaster-retaining structure, consisting of surrounding walls and sometimes a plywood base, around the prototype. Next, you seal the structure so that no plaster will leak out. Then you pour plaster over the prototype, covering it by approximately 1½ inches (3.8 cm).

Some molds are made by *frosting* the plaster instead of pouring it. This method is much like frosting a cake; the plaster is applied directly to the prototype and then shaped by hand and with tools to cover the prototype with an equal thickness of plaster all around. This method requires no plaster-retaining structure unless you plan to pour some of the plaster before frosting the rest.

If the prototype is square, or close to square, and if you plan to pour your mold, you'll use *cottles* (boards that are clamped together) to create the plaster-retaining structure (see photo 6 on page 23). For round and oval shapes, the structure consists of a wall made from aluminum roof flashing and a plywood base to which the flashing is fastened. To make the base, use a jigsaw to cut a piece of plywood in the rough shape of the base of the prototype; at any given point along its edge, the plywood should extend approximately 1½ inches

Wes Harvey

Ride a Long, 2006
11 x 6 x 6 inches (27.9 x 15.2 x 15.2 cm)
Press-molded stoneware and slip-cast porcelain;
electric fired, cone 6, reduction; cones 06 and 017
Photo by artist

Female sliding keys on the vertical edge of a mold section; female locking keys on the bottom edge

Wendy Walgate

Yellow Ahimsa Trophy, 2005
17 x 10 x 7 inches (43.2 x 25.4 x 17.8 cm)
Slip-cast white earthenware; cone 06;
postfired assembly
Photo by artist

(3.8 cm) beyond the edge of the prototype. To create the wall, just staple the flashing to the edge of the plywood (see photo 14 on page 39).

The height of the flashing will depend on the height of your prototype and on whether you'll be pouring the plaster or combining the pouring and frosting methods. Poured plaster must cover the prototype by 1½ inches (3.8 cm), so the flashing must be 1½ inches (3.8 cm) taller than the prototype. If you pour some of the plaster and then frost the upper portion of the prototype, the flashing needs to be only tall enough to retain the poured plaster; the frosted plaster will retain its own shape.

Both types of plaster-retaining structures—cottles and flashing—must be sealed so that liquid plaster doesn't leak out through any small openings. To seal the openings at the bottom of the structure, press a coil of soft clay into them (see photo 15 on page 39). Use duct tape to seal the vertical seam where the ends of the flashing meet; use clay coils to seal the exterior vertical corners where cottle boards meet.

To make a two-piece mold, you'll pour or frost one section of the prototype first, then pour the second section. Before pouring or frosting the first section, you'll protect the area of the prototype that you don't wish to cover with plaster yet by covering it with *blocking clay;* only the exposed area of the prototype will be covered by plaster. (Blocking clay, also called *modeling* or *plastic clay,* is very smooth white earthenware that is often used to create prototypes.) Once you've poured or frosted the first mold section and the plaster has set, you'll remove the blocking clay and pour the second section of the mold. Multiple-piece molds

are made in the same way; different areas of the prototype are protected with blocking clay before each mold section is poured.

When the poured or frosted plaster has set, the plaster-retaining structure is disassembled, the prototype is removed from the mold, and the mold is cleaned and dried.

creating keys

When you make a mold that consists of more than one piece, you must pour the pieces one at a time, letting each one set before the next is poured. When the finished mold is assembled, in preparation for casting, the sections must fit together exactly. To ensure their exact registration, you'll create *keys* in the mold as you make it. Keys are male and female fittings that ensure that the assembled mold pieces will register exactly.

Two kinds of keys exist: *locking keys* and *sliding keys* (see photo 8). Locking keys are the most common. To create the female portion of a locking key, you'll cut round divots in one section of the mold before the next section is poured. The new pour fills in these divots to form the male keys. When the mold is separated and reassembled, the keys fit together to ensure exact registration.

Sliding keys are used when one mold section must slide away from another. They're cone shaped, with rounded tips. The female portions of sliding keys are cut into the mold with a trimming tool and wood chisel, then sanded with wet/dry sandpaper. Make sure that the female key isn't undercut; once it starts flaring out, it should continue to do so.

soaping plaster

Using *mold soap* (a sealant made for molds) is absolutely necessary when you pour plaster on plaster—as you do when you make molds that consist of more than one piece, and when you use plaster prototypes. Forgetting to apply soap will cause the new plaster to stick to the previously poured plaster. Because mold soap contains oil and permeates the surface of the mold, it also prevents the previously poured plaster from absorbing water from the newly poured plaster. If you've soaped a mold and left it overnight, soap it again in the morning; water in the mold will begin to break down the soap after a few hours. If you've soaped a plaster prototype or mold and blocked it in with clay, the water and chemistry of the clay will also break down the soap. For more infor-

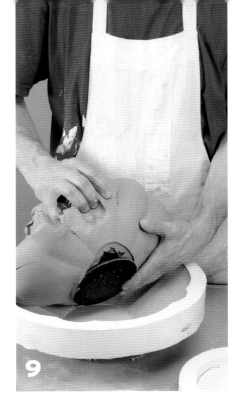

9

Removing a clay prototype

10

Deciding where to make a hole in the template

mation on soaping molds, see pages 21–22 and 32. To seal hardboard and cottles, I apply a spray lubricant to them before pouring plaster.

removing the prototype

Removing the prototype from the mold is one of the last things to do before drying the mold and preparing it for casting. Don't remove the prototype until the last section of the mold is cured. If the prototype is clay, removal is quite easy (see photo 9). Use a loop

tool to begin digging the clay out of the mold, taking care not to scrape the casting surface of the mold. If the clay is hard or you're concerned about damaging the mold, either pour water into the recess that you've already carved in the clay or submerge the mold in water. Soon the clay will soften and slide out of the mold easily. Use a medium-stiff brush (any brush will do except one with metal bristles) to loosen small bits of clay caught in any detailed areas of the mold.

Judith Salomon

Tumblers on Green Base, 2005
8 x 7 x 13 inches (20.3 x 17.8 x 33 cm)
Slip cast and hand built; cone 04
Photo by Anthony Gray

To remove prototypes made with templates, start by scraping off any plaster that may have run under them. If you've predrilled finger holes in a template, insert a screwdriver into one of them and use it to gradually pry up the template's edge; move from hole to hole until the template is loose. If you pry it up too quickly, you may chip the mold. Once the template is loose, the rest of the prototype will come out without difficulty.

If you haven't predrilled holes in the template, you can make holes while the template is still on the mold. To remove the template, first measure about 1 or 2 inches (2.5 or 5.1 cm) in from the edge of the mold (see photo 10 on page 17). Then carefully hammer the tip of a screwdriver into the template, and repeat to make four to six holes. Alternatively, use a ½-inch (1.3 cm) drill bit to do the same thing. Be very careful not to hit the mold with the screwdriver or drill bit. (For help repairing chipped molds, see page 145.)

Removing a plaster prototype from a mold can be either a blessing or a curse. On the one hand, if the proto-

type has no undercuts, it will usually separate from your mold easily. On the other hand, plaster prototypes are the most likely to stick to a mold—sometimes permanently! If a plaster prototype doesn't release easily from a one-piece mold, use a rubber mallet to hit the mold, striking the mold in the opposite direction to the one in which you want the prototype to move. For example, if you want the prototype to move south, strike the mold to drive it north.

separating mold sections that stick together

The sections of any multiple-piece mold have the potential to stick together, no matter what type of prototype you use and even if you've used the techniques I've just described. Sometimes the clay or plaster prototype sticks to the mold, so you have to pry the mold sections apart. For this task I use an industrial pastry scraper with a plastic handle and a stainless-steel blade that can withstand heavy abuse (see photo 11). Hammer the blade into the seam of the mold to a depth of ½ to ¾ inch (1.3 to 1.9 cm). Be careful not to drive

11

Prying the mold sections apart

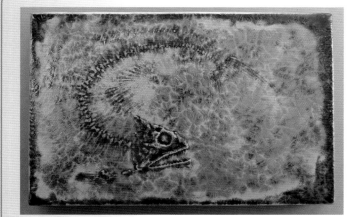

Bruce Gholson

Fossil Fish, 2006
12 x 8 x 1¾ inches (30.5 x 20.3 x 4.4 cm)
Slip-cast porcelain, one-piece plaster mold; slip-trailed imagery, multiple molybdenum and crystalline glazes; electric kiln, cone 8
Photo by artist

the scraper in too far; you may inadvertently cut off the keys. Push on the handle to apply leverage to the seam until the mold sections separate.

Do everything you can to separate the sections. If you fail, you'll have to break the mold and remake it. In this situation, make cuts in the mold and break it loose from the prototype. Inspect the prototype for undercuts and for areas of the mold and prototype that may have stuck together. Finally, after making adjustments to the prototype and soaping it, remake the mold.

cleaning & drying plaster molds

Finishing procedures are the same for all molds, although one-piece molds won't have mold soap on them. Remove the mold soap and mold release by scrubbing the mold with a sponge and white vinegar. Scrubbing will give you an opportunity to locate any areas that are still sealed and therefore repel water. Continue to work the area with a sponge and white vinegar until the plaster loses its nonabsorbency.

Next, shave the edges and corners of the new mold with a Surform tool. Then sand the whole exterior, first with coarse and then with fine wet/dry sandpaper. Sand the interior surfaces as well, removing the roughness left on the casting surface by the prototype. Finish the sanding with 600-grit sandpaper. Be careful not to sand the surfaces of mold sections that will interface when the mold is assembled for casting. If you alter these surfaces, the casting slip will ooze between the seams and leave fettles on the casting.

Rinse the mold under water, using a sponge to remove any residual plaster. Band all the sections of the mold together for drying; sometimes mold sections will warp if they're dried separately. When the molds are nearly dry, they can be separated to complete the drying process.

Air and heat are the most important factors in drying molds. Moving air carries water off the mold surface as the capillaries in the plaster transfer water from inside the mold. Dry your new molds with a fan. Some potters also use heat-drying methods such as placing molds in a drybox or setting them on or in a warm kiln. Dryboxes can be expensive to operate, so I use fans, even though they take a little longer. I also avoid using kiln tops—and especially kiln interiors—because kilns can destroy molds. Heating your molds to more than 125°F (52°C) will cause the plaster to lose its ability to absorb water; the molds will appear to be fine but will actually be unusable.

Paul McMullan

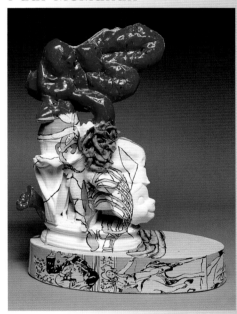

Boy & Girl, 2005
22 x 15 x 8 inches (55.9 x 38.1 x 20.3 cm)
Slip cast, slab built; underglaze, cone 04; glaze fired, oxidation
Photo by Jerry Mathieson

Amy M. Santoferraro

Deer Head, 2006
20 x 15 x 15 inches (50.8 x 38.1 x 38.1 cm)
Slip-cast porcelain; electric fired, cone 6; felt
and spray paint
Photo by artist

Using good tools and materials
is critical to any creative
endeavor. Using the right tools
can sometimes sharpen your
technical abilities instantly! In
this section you'll find descriptions of the tools and supplies
you're most likely to need for
mold making and slip casting, as
well as a few specific tools that
I recommend acquiring, such as
a jigsaw and carpenter's
squares. You'll also want to
have on hand some basic studio
supplies, such as needle tools,
sponges, buckets, and scales.

MOLD-MAKING MATERIALS & SUPPLIES

To make prototypes, I use readily available low-fire white clay, which is composed of 50 percent *ball clay* and 50
percent *talc.* (Ball clay is a sedimentary
clay containing kaolinite, mica, other
minerals, and organic matter. Talc is a
fine-grained mineral used as a *flux* in
low-fire bodies.) Because low-fire white
clay is smooth, it's easy to use for modeling finely detailed forms. For prototypes of handles and spouts, I also use
plastilene, an oil-based clay that's available at most art supply stores and that
comes in a variety of grades, from soft
to very firm.

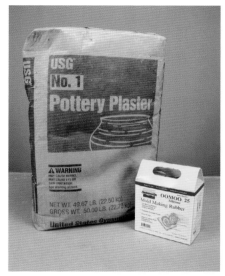

Plaster and rubber for making molds and master molds

A jigsaw, drill, and nail gun

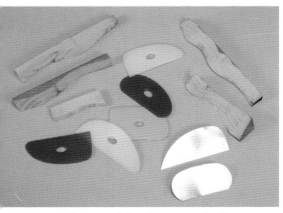

Commercial and homemade ribs

To make slip-casting molds, I use #1 Pottery Plaster, manufactured by U.S. Gypsum, because it's specifically engineered for this process and is also widely available. (See pages 26–27) for descriptions of this and other plasters.)

For making plaster *master molds* (positives used to produce *working molds*—the molds used for production), I use Hydrocal gypsum cement, which is also widely available (see page 27). To make rubber master molds from which I can produce working molds, I use a very durable rubber. Check with your ceramic supplier for recommended brands of rubber.

To model clay prototypes, I cut templates out of hardboard. The best type of hardboard is the kind from which clipboards are made; it's tempered, smooth on two sides, and very hard, and it withstands the abuse of the mold-making process well. Purchase the highest-quality hardboard available; it can be used many times without warping and will keep its sharp edges. Most lumberyards will special order high-quality hardboard for you.

You'll need a variety of adhesives. I use temporary spray adhesive to glue templates together, wood glue for gluing molds, and PC-11 epoxy for heavier jobs.

Whenever you pour plaster onto plaster—for example, when you're casting multiple-piece molds, using a plaster prototype, or making a plaster master mold—you must first coat the set plaster with mold soap. This sealant will prevent the new pour from sticking,

Ron Nagle

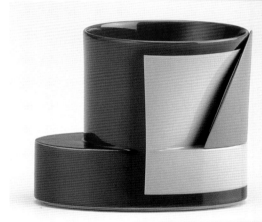

Bits of Schnittke, 2005
3 ¾ x 4 ¼ x 3 ¼ inches (9.5 x 10.8 x 8.3 cm)
Slip-cast earthenware; overglaze, decal
Photo by Don Tuttle

enabling you to separate the two plaster surfaces from each other when the new pour has set. Commercial mold soap can be purchased from your ceramic supplier premixed or as a paste that you dissolve in hot water. An excellent, readily available substitute is commercial oil soap, which you'll find among household cleaning supplies at large retail stores. Before I pour plaster, I also apply a spray mold release (available from ceramic or sculpture supply houses) to the mold and a spray lubricant to hardboard and cottles. To remove mold soap, use white vinegar.

You'll need wet/dry sandpaper to finish the surfaces of plaster molds.

MOLD-MAKING TOOLS & EQUIPMENT

A variable-speed drill with a mixing attachment is critical for mixing bubble-free plaster. Check your local hardware store for a mortar-mixing attachment. If you plan to mix your own slip, buy two of these. Each one comes with two blades, but for mixing plaster, you'll remove the upper blade. An important tip: Never use your plaster-mixing blade to mix anything except

plaster. Plaster that gets into clay can cause a *spit out* in low-fire clay bodies, and in high-fire clays, it can melt, leaving a hole in the finished piece.

I use a jigsaw to cut out my hardboard templates. Always use a very narrow finish blade with fine teeth so that you can cut sharp corners. A nail gun or hammer will help you assemble the templates.

You'll need a flat, nonporous surface on which to pour plaster; the section of a countertop that is cut out to make room for a sink makes an excellent one. Its slick surface makes removal of hardened plaster easy and also provides a smooth mold surface. I use pieces that I get from kitchen-counter suppliers. You can sometimes get these for free, but you may have to pay for scraps of the most expensive brands of plastic composites.

A pastry scraper is useful for scraping plaster and slip from everything in the studio. I also use it to pry molds apart.

To make a simple tool for cutting slabs from a block of clay (see photo 2 on page 37), cut two blocks from a sec-

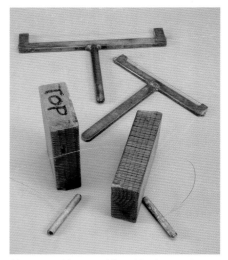

Cheese cutters, cutting blocks, and wire tool

tion of 2 x 4 (3.8 x 8.9 cm) lumber, nail them together temporarily, and cut a series of ⅜-inch-deep (1 cm) notches on one edge. Pull out the nails and separate the two blocks. To use this tool, stretch a guitar string or comparable wire across the blocks, fitting the wire ends into corresponding notches, and slide the blocks across the table, near the bottom of the prototype, to level the bottom of the form.

I've created a custom-made cutter for carving keys in a mold. An ordinary spoon can serve the same purpose. For instructions on making keys, see pages 16–17.

Craig Clifford

The Hunt, 2005
19 x 22 x 10 inches (48.3 x 55.9 x 25.4 cm)
Slip cast and press molded; electric fired, cone 04
Photo by artist

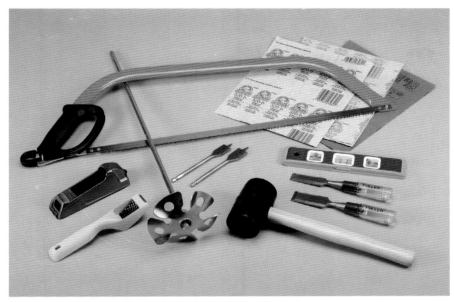

Bow saw, wet/dry sandpaper, torpedo level, chisels, rubber mallet, mortar-mixing attachment, Surform shaver and planer, and spade bits.

To create round and oval forms, use either aluminum roof flashing or tarpaper (available from building suppliers). Flashing is more rigid and leaves the finished plaster with a very clean surface. Tarpaper can be cut, folded, and secured with duct tape to fit around spherical forms. When you make round forms, you'll need to staple the flashing or tarpaper to a plywood base or to the plaster mold itself, so keep a staple gun on hand, too.

A torpedo level (a small bubble level), used with a board, will enable you to level soft plaster when you frost a mold. (Frosting is the process of applying plaster to a mold by hand rather than pouring the plaster into cottles or flashing. See page 31.)

A bow saw is useful for cutting excess plaster from molds in order to reduce their weight. Although you can do without them, chisels are handy for carving plaster from molds and from plaster prototypes. You'll find that a rubber mallet will help with mold disassembly and plaster prototype removal.

For carving No-Model Molds (see pages 91–92), I use a wood rasp. Surform tools, which are similar to rasps, are indispensable for shaving plaster. I depend on them for rounding corners and leveling surfaces on molds.

When I assemble templates, I use carpenter's squares to ensure that one template is exactly aligned with another. I also use them for squaring forms for pouring tiles.

Commercial ribs are used in slip casting to model clay prototypes. I prefer the well-known multicolored rubber ribs sold by ceramic suppliers because they come in a variety of firmnesses, from soft to hard, and are therefore excellent for modeling any type of complex curve. Still, commercial ribs are limited in their variety of curves, so I've made some of my own by cutting pieces of hardboard or redwood.

Cottles are boards that are clamped into a box shape; they serve to contain liquid plaster until it turns solid. Several sets consisting of different lengths and heights will prove useful. To make a set, first cut four lengths of plywood, making sure that their ends are square. Then cut blocks of 2 x 2-inch (5.1 x 5.1 cm) wood, as long as each piece of plywood is wide, making sure that the blocks are square as well. Apply wood glue to a block, position it flush with one end of a plywood length, and clamp the pieces together. Repeat to make the other cottles. For additional strength, drive screws through the plywood and into the block. Apply several layers of polyurethane to your cottles to keep them from warping. Purchase C-clamps at any hardware store. I prefer clamps with deep throats because they can grip the cottles closer to the bottom of the board, where the pressure of the liquid plaster is greatest.

Cottle boards assembled with C-clamps

Rain Harris

***Pasha**, 2003*
12 x 12 x 8 inches (30.5 x 30.5 x 20.3 cm)
Slip cast and altered; cone 6; luster
Photo by John Carland

optional mold-making tools & equipment

To assemble your templates, you can use a hot-glue gun instead of nails.

To trim excess clay from my template prototypes, I tried using a cheese cutter that I'd bought at a grocery store, but the cutter was very small and didn't remove much clay. I wanted a larger tool, so I had a machine shop make some jumbo cheese cutters for me. A guitar string or commercial cutting wire attached to a base shaped like a buck saw works almost as well. I made my cutter from a length of 1 x 2 (1.9 x 3.8 cm) lumber, a turnbuckle, a coat hanger, and a guitar string.

Spade bits, available at any hardware store, are useful for drilling holes in plaster. I use these bits to prepare broken molds for repair.

I use a compass and protractor for designing round forms that are divided into sections. Because I needed to draw large circles for platters, I created a custom compass from two pieces of 1 x 1 (1.9 x 1.9 cm) lumber, held together with a bolt. I cut a channel in the end of one piece to hold a pencil and created a pivot by using epoxy to glue a nail onto the other piece.

Plaster draws all the moisture from your skin, so protect your hands from constant chafing by wearing thin rubber or latex gloves when you mix it.

SLIP-CASTING MATERIALS & SUPPLIES

The primary slip-casting materials are casting slip and *deflocculant* (a soluble alkali that keeps the clay particles in suspension). Casting slip is a liquid mixture of 100 parts powdered clay to 40 parts water, with an added deflocculant.

You can purchase premixed casting slip. If you want to make your own, take a look at my slip recipe (see page 151), as well as the chapter on slip formulation (see pages 116–126) before buying deflocculant or mixing your slip. Test purchased slip to make sure it works in your molds. Even commercial slip varies from batch to batch; you may need to adjust the *viscosity* with water or deflocculant.

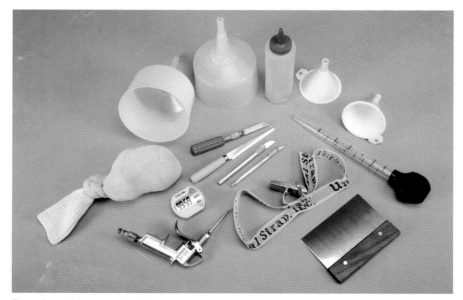

Funnels and squeeze bottle, baster, pastry scraper, mold strap, blowgun, timer, dusting sock, and craft and fettling knives.

SLIP-CASTING TOOLS & EQUIPMENT

When you mix slips and glazes, you'll need a separate mortar-mixing attachment to use with your variable-speed drill—a blade that you never use to mix plaster. Leave both mixing blades on the shaft when you mix slip.

I keep a variety of plastic funnels on hand to use when I cast certain types of molds. Buy spill-proof cylindrical funnels instead of cone-shaped ones; they hold more slip and are better at preventing spills. I've found cylindrical funnels through online photography equipment suppliers. I also use plastic tubing to create pour holes in some molds.

Heavy, wide rubber bands and nylon belts, available from ceramic suppliers, are used to bind multiple-piece molds together for casting. Rubber bands work with small molds, whereas larger molds require nylon belts.

During casting you'll use wood shims to prop up molds that aren't level. I use a jigsaw to cut shim wedges of various lengths from 1 x 2 (1.9 x 3.8 cm) lumber.

Fettling knives are standard pottery tools and are used to trim pour-hole waste and remove mold marks from castings. Before using them on slip-cast pieces that haven't yet dried, sharpen their edges with a bench grinder because they'll tear the clay if they're dull. To cut excess clay from castings, I use craft knives. To cut spouts, I use the ones with long, straight blades. They're excellent tools because they never tear the castings.

Squeeze bottles are useful for filling small molds; they also work well for vacuuming excess slip from the casting after a mold has been drained. Buy heavy-duty squeeze bottles from a beauty supply store; they create more

A hydrometer and a viscosimeter

suction than lightweight ones. A turkey baster will also work.

An electronic timer is indispensable for keeping track of the casting of several molds simultaneously so that you drain the molds on time. I use one that clips onto my clothing.

To *dust* molds in order to prevent a casting from sticking, I use white gym socks that I've filled with *nepheline syenite* (soda feldspar), baby powder, or a *calcined* casting body that I call *Chinese dust,* which I learned how to make from a book on Chinese ceramics. For instructions on how to make this dust, see page 139.

optional slip-casting tools & equipment

A *blunger,* either homemade or commercial, is a motorized slip mixer used to mix large batches of slip. It isn't absolutely necessary, but it does allow you to eliminate all the tiny air bubbles by mixing your slip for many hours.

If you're mixing slip for the first time, you may want to buy a *viscosimeter* (see the photo above) from your ceramic supplier. This instrument measures the viscosity of liquid slip, which determines the rate at which the slip will flow. Alternatively, you can measure viscosity by eye and hand, as I do (see page 125). You may also want to purchase a hydrometer to help you check the *specific gravity* of slip, although I don't use one myself. (Specific gravity is the ratio

of the weight of the slip to the weight of water.)

To release a casting from a mold, you can place your lips near the edge of the casting and blow between the casting and the mold—or you can use an air compressor.

Occasionally I use a wet/dry vacuum to remove casting slip from molds. Wash its compartment, hoses, and filter after every use so that you can reuse the slip you collect without polluting it.

SAFETY IN THE STUDIO

The primary safety concern for ceramists is the respiratory risk presented by inhaling airborne particles of clay, plaster, and glaze materials. Protect your health by following the guidelines below.

Your work space must be well ventilated. A powerful fan set within a window will draw a great deal of dust out of the studio—but only if you remember to turn it on whenever you're handling potentially dangerous materials. Your kiln must be accompanied by an adequate ventilation system, in order to protect you from the fumes produced by firing.

Wear an efficient respirator whenever you work with powdered substances.

If you have any cuts or scratches, cover them as needed. Wear gloves to protect your hands and cover any broken skin with bandages and clothing.

Make sure that all areas of your work space, including work surfaces, floors, and walls, are made from washable materials. Wipe them down frequently.

Take a shower as soon as your workday is through and wash your clothing right away, too. The less dust you track into your living space, the better.

plaster

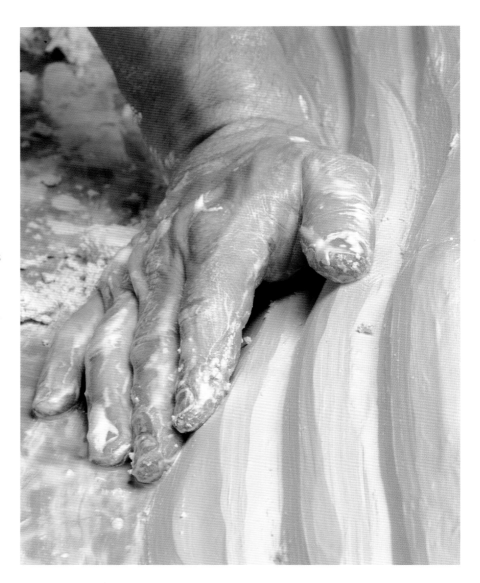

Plaster comes from gypsum, a naturally occurring mineral, and is mined, ground, calcined, and processed to perform in a vast array of applications, from pottery to the medical and construction fields. U.S. Gypsum is the primary producer of plasters in North America. Potters can easily and reliably use their products. Because the company has done all the technical calculations, the average studio potter can use plaster and plaster molds in creative ways without having to learn a great deal of technical information.

TYPES OF PLASTER

Different brands and types of plaster can be purchased from most local ceramic suppliers, and sometimes from building suppliers or sand and gravel yards. The following comments are based on my experience in the studio and on product literature.

#1 pottery plaster

U.S. Gypsum's #1 Pottery Plaster is the industry standard for slip casting and is also the best plaster for general studio uses. This plaster is formulated to deliver stronger, longer-lasting molds than any other type and is the best I have found. If you're going to use only one plaster, choose this one.

pottery plaster

The general-purpose product recommended for most slip-casting applications is Pottery Plaster (from U.S. Gypsum). For making pottery molds, this is my second choice after #1 Pottery Plaster.

molding plaster

Often referred to as "plaster of Paris" or "soft plaster" or, on the West Coast of the United States, "casting plaster," this material from U.S. Gypsum is a good one for making temporary patterns and for making waste molds (those used in intermediate molding processes and eventually thrown away), where expansion control, surface hardness, and strength are not of major importance.

puritan pottery plaster

Also made by U.S. Gypsum, this unique plaster, available with or without thermal shock additive, is designed for use with mechanical clay-forming machinery. It is absolutely the hardest, most wear-resistant plaster made for molds.

hydrocal gypsum cement

Gypsum cements are mixed and set like plaster but are as hard as cement. Many are used for tooling applications. Several types of gypsum cement exist; Hydrocal, Hydro-Stone, and Ultracal are the most commonly available. I use Hydrocal to make prototypes for tiles. Check with your supplier to determine the specifications, or contact the manufacturer.

WHAT DOES PLASTER DO?

Plaster "drinks" water. A plaster mold is similar to a large rigid sponge; it moves water from the surface into the mass. Plaster molds used for slip casting absorb water from the slip at a consistent rate throughout the mold. The ratio of plaster to water initially used to make the mold determines its water absorption rate. The longer a casting slip sits in a mold, the thicker the casting (i.e., the solidified slip) becomes. When the desired thickness is achieved, the excess slip is drained out of the mold. The remaining slip continues to dry and shrink away from the mold interior. As soon as the casting is firm enough to retain its shape, it is removed from the mold for drying.

Plaster manufacturers recommend the proper ratio of water to plaster or gypsum cement for making slip molds. When using Hydrocal, for example, the mix should be as dense as possible. Most manufacturers recommend a *consistency* of 45 pounds (20.4 kg) of water mixed with 100 pounds (45.4 kg) of gypsum cement. The consistency number, in this case 45, denotes the parts—by weight—of water to which 100 parts—by weight—of plaster or gypsum cement must be added in order to achieve the correct absorption rate.

The recommended consistency for making slip-casting molds with #1 Pottery Plaster is 70 pounds (31.8 kg) of water mixed with 100 pounds (45.4 kg) of plaster. This consistency will produce the correct water absorption rate for slip molds and is also excellent for most general applications.

If you were to inspect a piece of dried plaster under an electron microscope, you would see a field of evenly spaced crystals. The size of the openings between the crystals is determined by the ratio of plaster to water. The higher the ratio, the larger the spaces between the crystals and, to a point, the higher the absorption rate.

CALCULATING PLASTER AMOUNTS

How does a manufacturer's recommended consistency relate to a practical studio application? Using the recommended consistency of 70 for #1 Pottery Plaster, you'd mix 2.85 pounds (1.3 kg) of plaster into 1 quart (.95 L or 2 pounds) of water. I round up the weight of the plaster and mix 3 pounds (1.4 kg) of plaster into 1 quart (.95 L) of water. In other words, I mix three parts plaster to two parts water by weight. Even though this changes the consistency from 70 to 66, I've used this ratio successfully for years. It works fine, and the measurements and calculations are very easy.

Mixing the amounts just described will yield 80 cubic inches (1.3 L) of set plaster. To calculate the volume you plan to fill, use the formulas in

Charles B. Nalle

The Purse Teapot, 2005
11 x 12 x 4 inches (27.9 x 30.5 x 10.2 cm)
Three-piece mold cast; dipped and exterior sprayed; single fired, cone 6
Photo by David Coulter

Maryann Webster

Endangered Earth Reliquary, 2005
13 x 11 x 8 inches (33 x 27.9 x 20.3 cm)
Slip-cast porcelain; electric fired, cone 5; vitreous enamels, cone O19
Photo by Craig Law

FOR A RECTANGULAR SHAPE
Let's assume that you want to make a rectangular plaster wedging board (a board that plastic clay is kneaded on). The volume of a rectangular shape equals its length multiplied by its width multiplied by its height. For a rectangular shape that is 15 x 10 x 3 inches (38.1 x 25.4 x 7.6 cm), calculate its volume as follows:

15 x 10 x 3 inches (38.1 x 25.4 x 7.6 cm)= 450 cubic inches (7.4 L). You'll need 450 cubic inches (7.4 L) of liquid plaster to make this board.

Divide the volume by 80 to find the number of quarts of water you'll need in order to make enough plaster.

$$\frac{450 \text{ cubic inches (7.4 L)}}{80} = 5.6 \text{ quarts (5.3 L)}$$

Round the result up to 6; you'll need 6 quarts (5.7 L) of water.

To determine the weight of plaster you'll need, multiply the number of quarts or liters of water by 3 (the parts, by weight, of plaster required for each quart—or 2 pounds—(or one liter [1 kg] of water).

$$6 \times 3 = 18$$

You'll need 18 pounds (8.2 kg) of plaster.

FOR A CYLINDRICAL SHAPE
The volume of a cylinder equals pi (3.14) x radius squared x height.

For a cylinder that is 10 inches (25.4 cm) in diameter and 6 inches (15.2 cm) high, calculate the volume as follows (the radius squared of 10 is 25, or 5 x 5):

3.14 (pi) x (5 x 5) x 6 inches = 471 cubic inches (7.7 L). You'll need 471 cubic inches (7.7 L) of liquid plaster to make this cylinder.

Divide the volume by 80 to find the number of quarts of water you'll need in order to make enough plaster.

$$\frac{471 \text{ cubic inches (7.7 L)}}{80} = 5.9 \text{ quarts (5.6 L)}$$

Round the result up to 6; you'll need 6 quarts (5.7 L) of water.

To determine the weight of plaster needed, multiply the number of quarts of water by 3 (the parts, by weight, of plaster required for each quart—or 2 pounds—(or one liter [1 kg] of water).

$$6 \times 3 = 18$$

You'll need 18 pounds (8.2 kg) of plaster.

1

Weighing the plaster

2

Sifting the plaster into the water

Calculating Plaster Volumes on the opposite page. You'll also find a handy list of the amounts of plaster and water required for commonly mixed volumes in Appendix A: Plaster-Mixing Ratios on page 151.

MIXING & POURING PLASTER

When most people first begin to use plaster, they fear it will set too soon, but plaster doesn't enter the setting cycle until the mixing begins, and it can soak up to 30 minutes in water prior to mixing. In its liquid form, plaster flows like heavy cream. Take a look at the chart below. Once the setting process begins, the plaster becomes *thixotropic;* that is, it begins to hold its shape to some degree but returns to a liquid state when shaken. About 15 minutes into the setting process, the plaster takes on a plastic texture and, like clay, can be modeled.

Soon afterward the plaster becomes too firm to model, although, at this stage, before the plaster begins to get warm, it's very easy to shave and shape with tools. If you've frosted a mold, this is a good time to remove some of the roughness left by the frosting process.

Finally, about 20 minutes after you've started to add the dry plaster to the water, the plaster enters a curing period during which it gets very hot. Don't try to move a mold as the plaster is heating up; it can crack or chip quite easily at this stage. Once the plaster has fully entered the heat cycle, disassemble the mold and remove any templates that you've incorporated in your prototypes. Plaster expands as it heats, so you're less likely to chip the edge of the rim of the mold's casting surface if you remove the templates now.

To mix plaster, start with a thoroughly cleaned bucket that is large enough to hold at least twice the volume of water necessary for the batch. (Once the plaster is added to a bucket with water in it, the bucket will be about 80 percent full.) Coat the bucket with a thin layer of petroleum jelly to help the mixed plaster release from it later. Then wash your hands with soap so you won't contaminate any molds.

Measure or weigh room-temperature water—about 70°F (21.1°C)—and place it in the bucket. If you want the plaster to expand less, use water up to 100°F (37.7°C), though in most cases this is unnecessary.

Weigh out the plaster and add it to the water by quickly sifting large handfuls of plaster through your fingers (see photos 1 and 2). When you've added all the plaster, scrape all dry plaster from the sides of the bucket into the water.

The plaster is now in the soaking period. (Although the plaster can rest in the water for up to 30 minutes prior to mixing, if you don't need to delay the mixing, the soaking period should last for about three minutes.) Bounce the bucket up and down to remove air bubbles carried in by the dry plaster. You may also hit the side of the bucket with your hand or kick it with your foot. Don't put your hand or the mixing attachment into the bucket until the plaster is fully soaked because mixing will start the setting process. With

time frames for plaster mixing & setting

	Add Plaster	Soak	Mix	Liquid	Thixotropic	Plastic	Hardening Cycle	Heat Cycle
Time (in Minutes)	1	3	3	3	2	3	5	10
Time Elapsed	1	4	7	10	12	15	20	30

small batches of plaster, the soaking time can be reduced as long as all the particles of plaster are well soaked.

Using a variable-speed drill with a propeller-type mixing attachment, mix the plaster for two to three minutes on high speed, with the shaft of the attachment tilted at an angle of about 15 degrees (see photo 3). Mix until the liquid is homogeneous. When I mix small batches, I use a 1-gallon (3.8 L) pitcher and a stick-type hand blender (see photo 4).

This mixing method yields the most consistent, bubble-free finished plaster. Your main objective is to release any air carried in by the plaster powder without creating a whirlpool in the mixture. You can mix plaster entirely by hand, but it's very difficult to remove the smallest bubbles this way. As the set plaster erodes slowly over the life of a mold, bubbles will appear on the mold's casting surface. The result will be a field of tiny bumps on your casting, which you'll have to sponge off before bisque firing.

Mix with your hand for the last minute, cupping your hand slightly and rotating it in the plaster with a brisk elliptical motion to draw plaster and air bubbles from the bottom of the bucket to the top. Air bubbles will gather on the surface and can be skimmed off into

Mixing the plaster

the trash. Finishing the mixing by hand will allow you to feel the plaster change from a watery mixture to a creamy one.

When you're mixing very large batches, you can extend the setting time in the liquid and plastic stages by adding a few ounces of white vinegar to the water before adding the plaster. This is especially useful when you're mak-

Use a hand blender for a small batch of plaster

ing a frosted mold (see the next section) or a large mold, or when sculpting forms in plaster.

If you're going to pour the plaster, you should do so as soon as it begins to change from watery to creamy. Place your hand inside the cottle boards or flashing, with the tips of your fingers touching or nearly touching the sides and your hand at a slight angle off vertical. Pour the plaster against your hand (see photo 26 on page 42). If your hand is in the correct position, the plaster will run down it and the sides of the cottles without splashing.

Shake the entire work surface to level the liquid within the cottles and to release any residual bubbles.

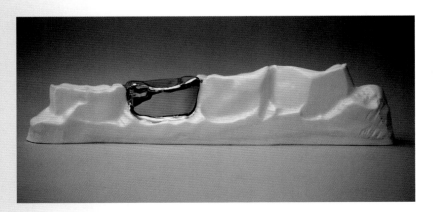

David Alban

Teeth, 2004
4 x 6 x 1 inches (10.2 x 15.2 x 2.5 cm)
Cast bone china; single fired, 2516°F (1380°C);
gold luster
Photo by artist

frosting

Frosting is a method of applying plaster by hand or with a tool such as a scraper and is similar to frosting a cake, except that you have a limited amount of time in which to finish. Begin by pouring plaster over the form while the plaster is still quite liquid. As the plaster begins to thicken, frost the form until the plaster is the same thickness all over. While the plaster is still in the plastic stage, check the thickness of the frosted layer by pushing your finger through to the surface of the prototype (see photo 7 on page 37). When you've achieved an even thickness, place a board with a torpedo level on top of the plaster. To create a flat, level bottom on your mold, press the board into the plaster, checking the level as you do.

MODELING A PLASTER PROTOTYPE BY HAND

Sometimes, when I've mixed too much plaster, I use the excess to model a prototype by hand. This is a technique that Tom Spleth uses to make many of his forms (see page 55–57). To model a plaster prototype, first pour the liquid plaster onto a smooth surface (see photo 5). As you model the plaster, you'll see it enter the thixotropic stage; the plaster will begin to hold its shape (see photo 6). When the plaster reaches this stage, you can begin to model it into the basic form.

Soon the plaster will enter the plastic stage, during which you can model and cut it easily (see photos 7 and 8). As the plaster sets, add water to its surface so that you can smooth it.

At a certain point, the plaster will become too hard to model; you can continue to shape it with hand tools. When you are finished, leave the prototype to set. Wait for the plaster to go through the full heat cycle before moving it from the table. Then you can evaluate the form (see photo 9). The

Pouring the liquid plaster onto the table

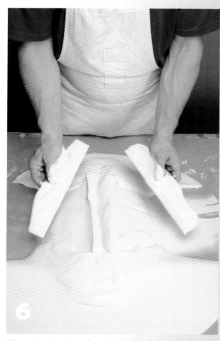

The plaster begins to hold its shape.

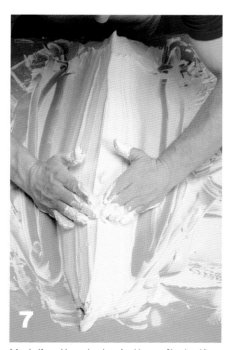

Modeling the plaster in the soft plastic stage

Sculpting plaster at a slightly firmer stage

9

Evaluating the finished plaster form

10

Applying mold soap with a sponge

11

Removing the excess soap with a clean sponge

chemical reaction during this heat cycle gives plaster its physical strength, much as tempering the blade of a knife makes it stronger.

APPLYING MOLD SOAP & OTHER SEPARATORS

To seal the plaster with mold soap, either massage the soap on by hand or apply it liberally with a sponge or brush (see photo 10). Let the plaster absorb the soap for one to two minutes and then remove the excess with a clean, damp sponge (see photo 11). Repeat this process four or five times, until you can see the water bead up as you remove the excess. If you have an air compressor with a blowgun, spread the soap in a thin layer by blowing air across the prototype after the last soaping. This will ensure that the prototype is fully sealed. To make separation even easier, apply a spray mold release over the last layer of soap.

When you create a mold from a found object that is made of metal, wood, or stone, spray the object first with a spray lubricant. (On nonabsorbent surfaces, apply it very lightly.) I apply spray lubricant to hardboard and to cottles, as well. The thin layer of oil will act as the separator. You can also use petroleum jelly by diluting it with 10 parts paint thinner to one part petroleum jelly.

For instructions on cleaning soaped molds, see page 19.

STORING PLASTER

Store your dry plaster in a dry area, away from the sink and a few inches off the ground. A board resting on a few bricks, or a section of pallet, will provide enough height. Cover open bags of plaster with plastic when they're not in use in order to keep ambient moisture to a minimum and to protect them from splashed water. Plaster that's been stored for a long time may absorb moisture from the air. When you put your hand in the bag, the dry plaster should feel smooth. If you feel small lumps, discard the plaster and buy more.

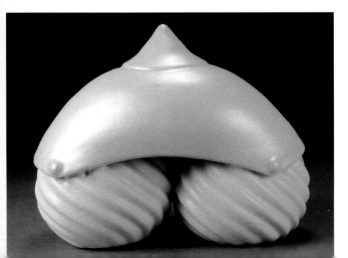

Lea Tyler

Armored Titty, 2006
5 x 6 x 3 inches (12.7 x 15.2 x 7.6 cm)
Slip-cast and thrown parts; electric fired, cone 6, oxidation; luster, cone 019
Photo by artist

Anne Kraus

a conversation with the materials

I Look for a Door, 1999
9 ¼ x 11 x 8 ¼ inches (23.5 x 27.9 x 21 cm)
Slip cast
Photo by artist
Courtesy of Garth Clark Gallery

Anne once said that she was coerced into mold making and slip casting, and went into the processes kicking and screaming. When she arrived at Alfred University, she postponed signing up for classes in order to avoid the crowds. By the time she went to register, all the classes were filled except for slip casting. She also had to take technical classes on clay and glaze chemistry, in which she was always asked to mix up the slip. (Students whose last names started with *K* were assigned to slip-casting recipes.) She never managed to get out of that assignment, so she was forced to learn how to mix different slips. "That's how it happened, that's how it started."

With casting, Anne found that a lot of her work was "blind"—she couldn't quite see where she was going or what the final result would be. "I do all this work, but I never quite know what anything will look like until I've actually cast it in slip, even after all the models I make."

During her first semester, Anne made some unsuccessful beginning molds, then one day just decided to make 10 molds at random. She found some objects in a classroom, made some models, cast them, and put the castings together in different ways, without any preconceived notions of the results. The experience was a turning point for her. Eventually her ambivalence about slip casting disappeared, and Anne became totally involved. In fact, she stopped attending all her other classes, but her instructors didn't seem to mind.

Anne felt that her creativity developed from a conversation with the materials and with the technique. "I wasn't the one; it wasn't totally my ballgame anymore." She'd try something out, wait and see what the slip or plaster did, and then respond. Her one-of-a-kind work is intensely decorated; she was never a traditional production potter. She even switched to hand building for a while because using a mold to make only three teapots took so much time. But she found that hand building didn't allow her to achieve the intricacy of shape she wanted. She spent extended periods of time developing her models, and she appreciated the fact that the mold-making process allowed her to keep those models damp for a week or more and to work on them without having to worry about their moisture content—a constant concern in hand building.

Even though she knew she'd spend weeks making a mold and then cast it only two or three times, from Anne's point of view, the time she spent was well worthwhile. "I know it's going to take a huge amount of time, but I also know that this shape and this whole give and take with the materials and the process works for me. Also, I love handling plaster."

Anne always experienced what she called a "heavy relationship" between the forms she conceived and the process of mold making. As she built a model, she'd be thinking about the making of the mold, the painting of her work, and all the other steps involved in producing a finished piece. She'd simultaneously be deciding how many pieces a mold would require, what the pieces would be shaped like, whether those pieces would actually be feasible, and whether she'd be able to separate parts of the mold easily. If she thought a piece was going to be too large, she'd have to decide how to turn it into two pieces, and if she made it in two pieces, about how she could change the shape to take advan-

Our Flight/Crash Site Dish Pair, 1997
13 ½ inches (34.3 cm)
Slip cast
Photo by artist
Courtesy of Garth Clark Gallery

tage of those additional pieces. "I usually start getting so complicated that I make a mistake. And that's when it gets interesting." She would even create models that were impossible to cast, make the molds, and then chisel away at their inner sur-

work reflected and accentuated her askew way of looking at the world. The content of her imagery, she explained, was about imbalance.

Anne saw herself as searching for a balance—an understanding—with her materials. "If there's a really good

"I usually start getting so complicated that I make a mistake. And that's when it gets interesting."

faces until they worked. "That was always Tom Spleth's favorite expression," she said: "It'll work."

For Anne, casting was never about control. Slip "has its own mentality, which to me is the attraction. Hand building doesn't have that for me. It's too forgiving. It'll do whatever you want, and that's the problem. There's not enough give and take the way there is with all the requirements in casting." Anne's models often looked symmetrical to her, for example, but she found that her castings sometimes weren't. She felt that her cast

communication or give and take with the materials, that's when the pieces work the best." She saw this process as perpetual, not as one with a conclusion—as a form of intimacy in which the artist and materials just get closer and closer. "The way I handle my work, the way I touch it—my hands just seem to become closer or more sensitive, or more forgiving. Because you have narrative and imagery, it's like reading a book."

She believed that her own desires and sense of the world were revealed in her forms. "A pot is a pot, but it's also something else—something far beyond the pot. Oh, it's a vase, a teapot, a teacup, but it's another thing." Anne described this other thing as the bounce back and forth between the common object and the not-so-common something going on inside of it. Production-type potters, she pointed out, often speak about what they want a piece to be—a sweetmeat tray, a fish plate. But what she wanted to say was, "It's a teapot, but watch out!" Never underestimate objects, she warned. Nothing is ever quite what you think it is. Her spiritual search and her "watch out" point of view were one and the same to Anne; her work was her way of acting them out.

Anne always felt strongly that education, especially in ceramics, was often too technically oriented. In her own work, the technical and artistic aspects were intertwined. "Only when they grow together do they develop this give and take—this kind of conversation that goes on with the materials." Technical information wasn't something she used; it was an integral part of her work. She never felt able to teach her own approach because she found that students wanted only technical information. But from Anne's point of view, when bits of scientific information weren't connected to something, they were completely meaningless. "You need to decide in your head to do something and ask yourself how to do it. And say, 'Okay, I'll try this.' And when it doesn't work, you say, 'Well, it didn't quite work, but this is kind of interesting, so I'll take that part of it, and I'll try something else.'

You know, always incorporating something from the materials."

Anne never had a role model in ceramics and didn't seek support from the ceramics community or from any other art community, but she did admire people who stepped out and did something different—people such as director and producer George Lucas, whose career she followed closely.

Unfortunately, Anne passed away in 2003. Like her pieces, she was one of a kind; even if you had the mold, you couldn't make a duplicate. I miss her curious humor and the stories in her work that spoke of the journey born from a life lived equally in the subjective, feeling world and in the objective, material world.

The Green Bridge Motel, 2001
40 x 28 ½ inches (101.6 x 72.4 cm)
Tiles mounted on wood
Photo by artist
Courtesy of Garth Clark Gallery

ANNE KRAUS'S work is included in numerous public collections, including the Los Angeles County Museum of Art; the Museum of Fine Arts, Houston; the Newark Museum; the Carnegie Museum of Art; the Everson Museum of Art; the International Ceramic Museum, Shigaraki, Japan; and the Victoria and Albert Museum in London. Kraus received her B.A. in painting in 1978 from the University of Pennsylvania, Philadelphia, and her B.F.A. in ceramics from the New York State College of Ceramics at Alfred University. In 1988 she was awarded the New Jersey State Council on the Arts Award. Her work has been featured and reviewed in various publications, including the *New York Times,* the *Los Angeles Times,* and *Ceramics: Art and Perception.*

Anne kept an active dream journal, a primary source for her art. She created narrative scenes on vessels, which she mixed with meticulously printed text. Together the scenes and text explore stories depicting man's tenuous balance between reality and the unknown. Large, wall-mounted tile pictures drenched in color had been the most recent developments in her work. Anne died in 2003 in Boulder, Colorado.

one-piece molds

one-piece molds

Easy-to-make one-piece molds are good places for beginning mold makers to start. I made my very simple first mold by covering a 1-inch-thick (2.5 cm) slab of clay with plaster. The first valuable mold-making lessons I learned were what an undercut is and how easily an undercut can trap a casting in a mold (see page 12). Because my mold had undercuts, I had to bang it repeatedly to remove the casting. I was just happy that the mold worked at all! Remember: One-piece mold prototypes always taper from wide at the top rim to narrow at the bottom and are always molded upside down. Forms that can be made with one-piece molds include tumblers, bowls, platters, plates, vases, and planters.

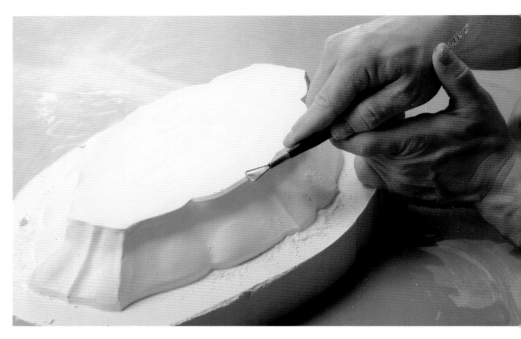

MAKING A CLAY PROTOTYPE BY HAND

The simplest way to make a one-piece mold is to shape *modeling clay* on a smooth, nonporous surface—a process that I call "mud on the table." Simple bowls, plates, and even large platters can be made in this manner. As for any forming process, you'll need a variety of pottery tools. Remember that you'll be shaping the exterior of the prototype upside down.

For rough forming, wet the clay with water and model it until it's the general proportion that you desire (see

Yasuyo Nishida

Cups—Stripescape, 2006
9 x 10 x 8 inches (22.9 x 25.4 x 20.3 cm)
Slip-cast porcelain; overglaze
Photo by artist

photo 1). In the example shown here, I'm making a serving dish. You will actually feel the form begin to emerge, just as you would on a potter's wheel. Next, using cutting blocks and a wire, level the top of the prototype, which will become the bottom of your cast piece (see photos 2 and 3). Finish the form by using sponges and ribs to create the final detail. Any small holes in the prototype will create small protrusions in the mold; these can be sanded off the finished mold. Remove any protrusions from the prototype, since these will show up as holes in the mold.

making the mold

Because I used the frosting method to mold this prototype, I drew a line on the work surface, as far away from the edges of the prototype as I wanted my mold to be thick (see photo 4). This line gave me a visual indication of how close my scraper could come to the prototype.

Pour plaster over the prototype (see photo 5). Then use a scraper to frost the plaster onto the form (see photo 6). To test the thickness of the plaster you're applying, push your finger into it until it touches the prototype (see photo 7). (Do this early on; if you do it during the setting stage, you may leave

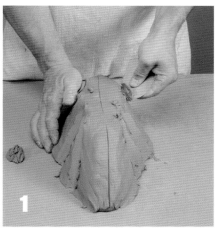

1

After wetting, begin shaping the form.

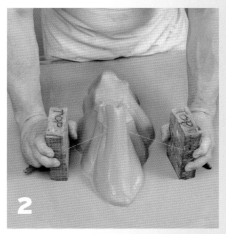

2

Leveling the bottom, using cutting blocks and a wire tool

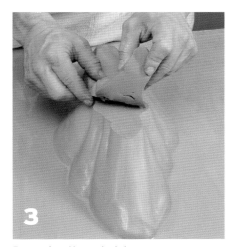

3

Removing the cut slab

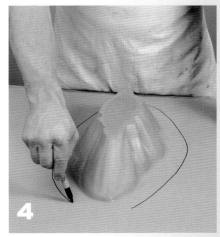

4

Marking the perimeter for the plaster mold

5

Pouring the plaster over the prototype

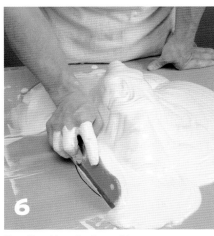

6

Frosting the plaster with a scraper

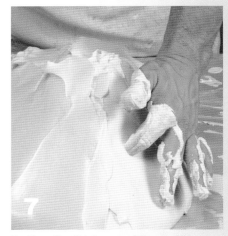

7

Testing the thickness of the mold

air pockets in the plaster.) Finally, while the plaster is still soft, level it with a board and a torpedo level (see photo 8). You'll feel the plaster go through the heat-setting cycle, which is described on pages 29-30. Remove the prototype from the finished mold after the plaster is set (see photo 9). When you're finished, clean and dry the mold (see page 19).

Leveling the bottom of the frosted mold

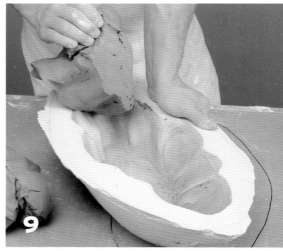

Removing the prototype

Rebecca Harvey

Torpedo, 2005
9 x 6 x 6 inches (22.9 x 15.2 x 15.2 cm)
Slip-cast and assembled porcelain; cone 6, oxidation
Photo by artist

Andrew Martin

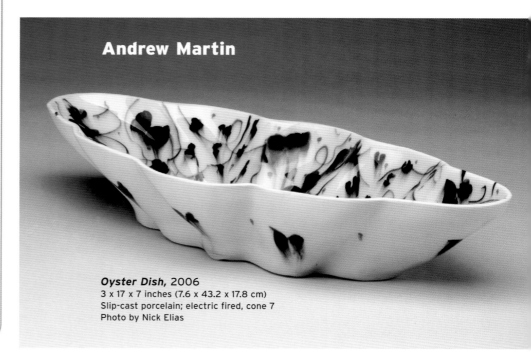

Oyster Dish, 2006
3 x 17 x 7 inches (7.6 x 43.2 x 17.8 cm)
Slip-cast porcelain; electric fired, cone 7
Photo by Nick Elias

USING ONE TEMPLATE TO MAKE A CLAY PROTOTYPE

Making a one-template prototype is similar to forming clay by hand except that the shape of the prototype's rim is determined before you start forming the clay. Start by cutting a hardboard template in the shape of the rim (see figure 1). Cover the template with packed clay. Place the template and clay on a piece of scrap wood or any level object that will raise them above your work surface. Then use a cheese cutter to cut away the clay until you've exposed the template's edge (see photo 10). Model the clay, as well (see photo 11). Don't rely on tools alone!

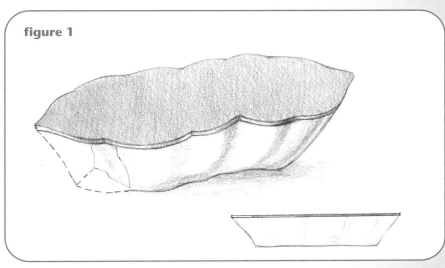

figure 1

10

Cutting against the template with a cheese cutter

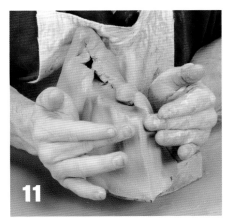

11

Modeling the prototype by hand

Now use cutting blocks and a wire to level the bottom of the prototype (see photo 12). (The bottom is actually the top of the clay form as you look down on it.) Smooth the form with ribs, and sponge its surface to remove any roughness (see photo 13).

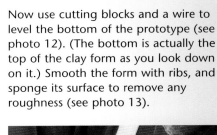

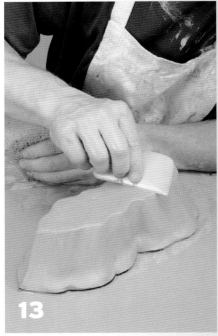

13

Smoothing the form with ribs

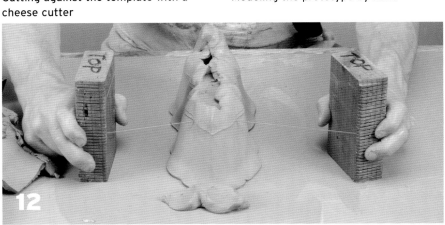

12

Using cutting blocks and a wire tool to level the bottom

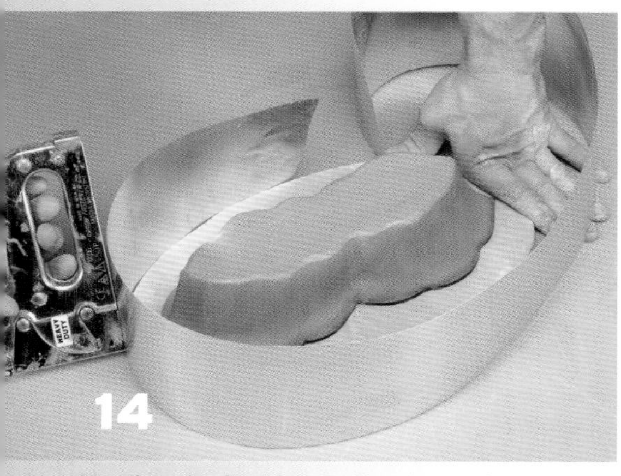

Stapling the flashing to the plywood

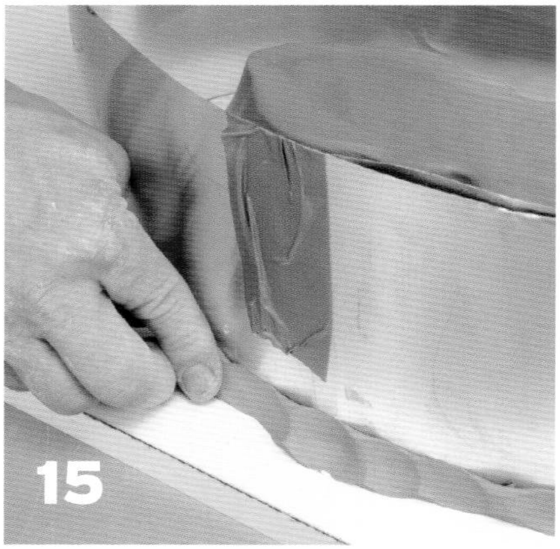

Sealing the flashing with coils of clay

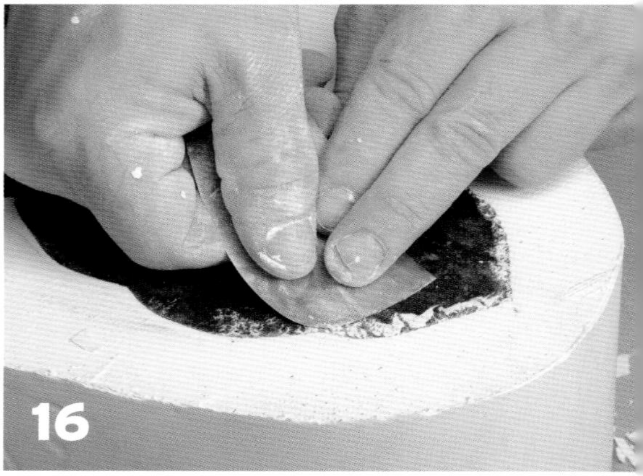

Scraping plaster off the template, up to its edge

making the mold

To make the mold, start by placing the prototype on a piece of plywood. Apply spray lubricant to the plywood and assemble flashing around the form (see photo 14). Seal the outer edge of the flashing with small coils of clay (see photo 15). Pour the plaster to cover the form by 1½ inches (3.8 cm).

When the plaster has set and while it's still hot, remove the flashing and the plywood board. If any plaster has run underneath the template, use a metal rib to scrape it away, up to the edge of the template (see photo 16). To remove the template, hammer a screwdriver through it, about 1 or 2 inches (2.5 or 5.1 cm) from the edge. Being careful not to drive the screwdriver into the plaster, gradually pry the template up until it breaks free of the mold (see photo 17). The basic process of removing templates is always the same. Just remember that you're least likely to chip the mold if you remove templates when the plaster is just past the peak of its heat cycle. Then remove the clay (see photo 18).

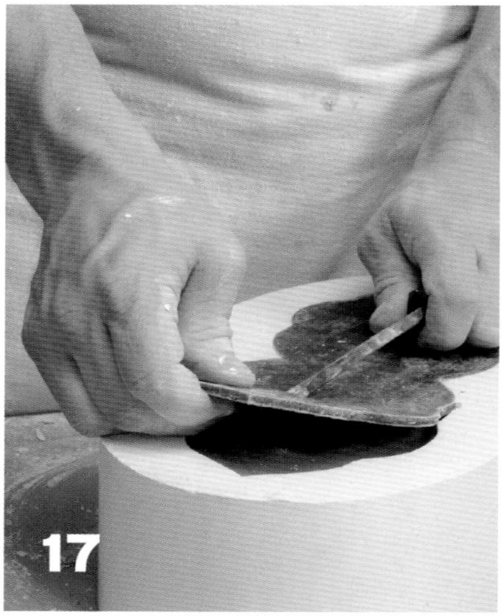

Prying up the template

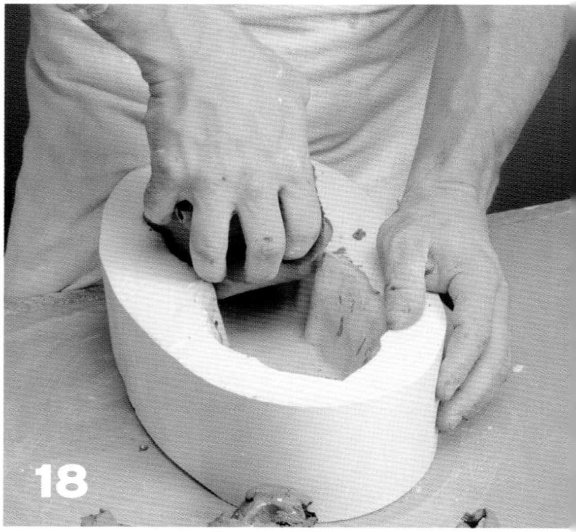

Removing the clay

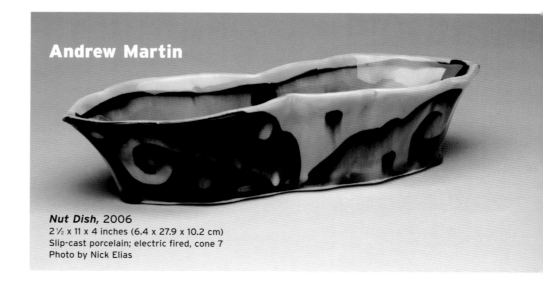

Andrew Martin

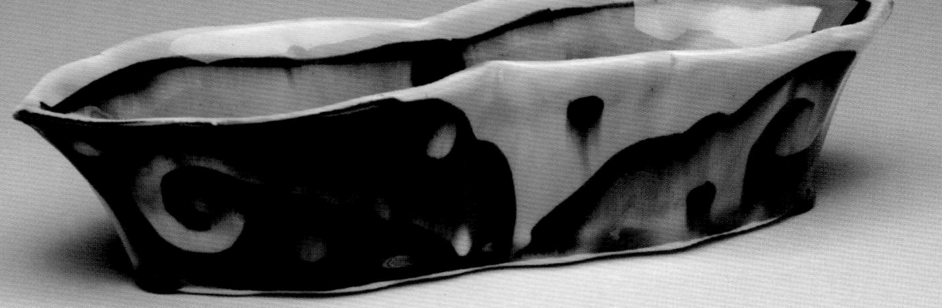

Nut Dish, 2006
2½ x 11 x 4 inches (6.4 x 27.9 x 10.2 cm)
Slip-cast porcelain; electric fired, cone 7
Photo by Nick Elias

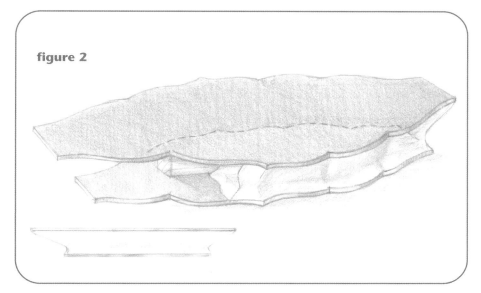

figure 2

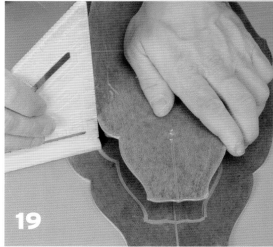

Using a carpenter's square to align the templates

USING TWO TEMPLATES TO MAKE A CLAY PROTOTYPE

The advantage to this method, which in this example I'm using to make a plate (see figure 2) is that you can determine the shape of both the rim and *footprint* (the shape of the portion of a pot that sits on the table), as well as the height of the form, before you make the prototype. The template process makes it easy to translate a drawing of the shape (top view) of a pot into an actual form.

Start by cutting the two templates and then drawing an outline of the footprint shape onto the underside of the rim template. In addition, draw lines across both templates to indicate how they should be aligned. I also mark small *x*s on both templates, for the same purpose. After determining the height of the form, I use the lines and the *x*s to realign the two templates.

The plate's height is determined by placing blocks of wood between the two templates; I use a combination of plywood, hardboard, and board lumber to get the spacing right. Assemble the templates and wood spacers by nailing the spacers inside the outline on the rim template. Then place the corner of a carpenter's square on the traced line on the rim template and align the foot template to the vertical edge of the square (see photo 19). When this is aligned, nail the floor template in place (see photo 20).

Nailing the floor template in place

41

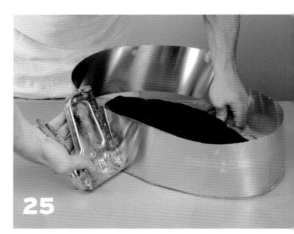

Once the prototype frame is complete, pack the space between the two templates with clay (see photo 21). When the frame is completely covered, place it on a piece of plaster so that you can reach the entire exterior as you shape the clay. Cut against the templates with a cheese cutter until the form is revealed (see photo 22). I model the prototype further with ribs and by hand (see photo 23). When the modeling is finished, the bottom of the prototype should be clean, and the edge of the rim template should be exposed and clean, as well.

making the mold

To make the mold, start by cutting a piece of plywood in the general shape of the mold, making it 1½ inches (3.8 cm) wider than the prototype. Place the prototype upside down on the plywood. Apply spray lubricant to the plywood (see photo 24). Then staple flashing around it (see photo 25). Tape the vertical seam of the flashing with duct tape and seal the seam at the bottom by pressing plastic clay around it. Pour the plaster (see photo 26). The plaster should cover the floor of the prototype by 1½ inches (3.8 cm).

When the plaster has reached the peak of the heat cycle, remove the flashing, flip the mold over, and remove the plywood. If any plaster has run under the rim template, scrape it off with a metal rib. (If you don't do this, the rim of the mold will chip as the template is removed.) To remove the prototype, hammer the tip of a screwdriver into the template, about 1 or 2 inches (2.5 or 5.1 cm) from the edge, being careful not to drive the screwdriver into the plaster. Then, using the screwdriver as a lever, gradually pry up the template (see photo 27). Slowly remove the template and the remainder of the prototype. Photo 28 shows the empty mold, ready for cleaning and drying.

Packing clay between the templates

Cutting against the template with a cheese cutter

Modeling the prototype with a rib

Spraying lubricant onto the plywood

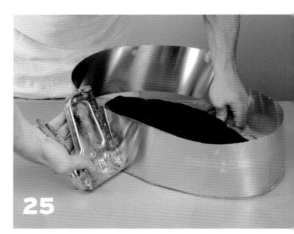
Stapling flashing to the plywood

Pouring the plaster

27

Prying up the template with a screwdriver

28

Checking the finished mold after removing the prototype

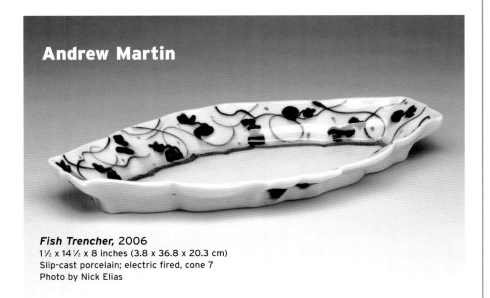

Andrew Martin

Fish Trencher, 2006
1½ x 14½ x 8 inches (3.8 x 36.8 x 20.3 cm)
Slip-cast porcelain; electric fired, cone 7
Photo by Nick Elias

Richard Shaw

Frog Vase, 1997
12 x 11 x 6½ inches (30.5 x 27.9 x 16.5 cm)
Slip-cast porcelain; glaze, cone 6
Photo by the Addison Gallery of American Art

Wes Harvey

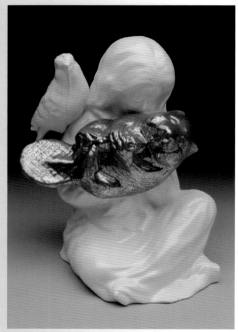

Madonna & Beaver, 2006
9 x 6 x 6 inches (22.9 x 15.2 x 15.2 cm)
Slip-cast porcelain; low-fire glaze with luster; electric fired, cones 06 and 017
Photo by artist

USING THREE TEMPLATES TO MAKE CLAY PROTOTYPES

three templates can be used to make footed forms such as bowls, vases, casseroles, teapots, serving dishes, platters, cups, and saucers. How to master the making of feet was an issue I skirted for years. When I finally decided to try casting feet, they ended up requiring a lot of cleanup because they were rough and inexact. But I knew that in a studio situation, they had to be made very efficiently and, for my aesthetic, very exactly. As in the case of lids, approximate wasn't good enough for me. As a result, I developed a system in which I use three hardboard templates. One is for the rim of the bowl and the other two are for the area where the body and foot meet (see figure 3).

I start by using spray adhesive to glue together two pieces of ⅛-inch-thick (.3 cm) hardboard. Then I cut out the shape and separate the glued hardboard pieces. One template is used to form the floor of the body and the other is used to form the foot. Because these two templates are cut out together, they're exact duplicates and always fit together perfectly.

Most feet can be made with one-piece molds. For heavier forms or for forms in which the foot spreads out as it descends from the bottom of the bowl to the table, use the double-walled, hollow-cast foot mold described on pages 88–89. The shape of the exterior foot provides an aesthetic appeal, while the interior wall bears the weight of the form above it. Without the interior wall, the exterior foot would be crushed under the weight of the body during firing.

figure 3

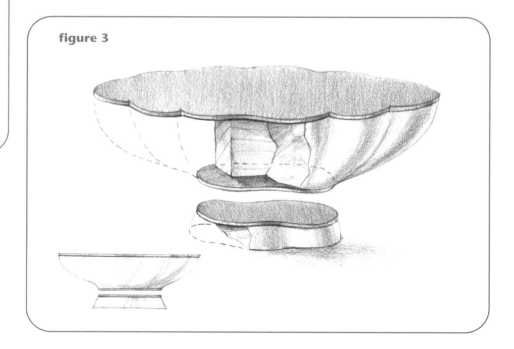

making footed bowls

Let's design two footed bowls that share one dimension as a constant— the size of the rim. Start by drawing a 14-inch-diameter (35.6 cm) circle on a piece of hardboard. Then, using a marker, divide the circle into sections, much as some Chinese or Islamic bowls are designed. (These bowls each have five small sections and five large sections, and each of the sections is lobed.) Next, use spray adhesive to bond this piece of hardboard to another. Then cut out the circle and separate the pieces of hardboard to get your two rim templates for the two bowls.

The foot of a bowl can be a variety of sizes, but if it's too small, you'll end up with a cone, and if it's too large, you'll have a cylinder. Somewhere in between is a range of sizes that will work. For these bowls, I made one foot 5½ inches (14 cm) in diameter and the other 7 inches (17.8 cm).

Cut two pairs of templates for the feet of both bowls, as described on the opposite page. If a foot is round, the two templates you cut for it will always align correctly. If they're any other shape, you'll need to mark these templates so that you can keep them aligned. In nonconcentric forms, you must make a registration mark so all the templates can be realigned during the mold-making process and later during the casting. I mark the templates with xs. (I've modeled the clay on the wrong side of the foot template a few times; the results were mirror images of the forms I actually needed.)

Now that you have your two sets of circles for the feet, lay one pair of circles over a rim template. Visualize the bowl upside down as you look at it

29

Packing clay around the first armature

from the bottom. You'll begin to see the relationship of the foot to the rim. Next, raise the templates up to help you visualize the curve between the rim and the foot.

Using a marker, trace the foot template shape onto the rim template. This traced line will help you align the rim and the floor correctly. With nonconcentric forms, make every effort to keep all the parts clearly marked.

Now mark one of the smaller templates "foot interface," and on its flip side, mark "foot-clay here." Mark its duplicate "bowl-interface" to indicate the floor of the bowl. Check to see that your marks are correct by placing the templates together. (Marking is not as critical on the templates for these two

bowls because the feet are concentric circles.)

After you've determined the heights of the two bowls, you'll use wood blocks as spacers between the rim and bowl-interface templates. Position a rim template on top of the wood blocks, making sure to position the blocks inside the traced line for the foot template. Leave the tracing exposed so you can align the bowl-interface template with the rim template. Nail the rim template to the blocks.

Turn the assembly over and use a carpenter's square to align the template for the floor of the bowl, then nail it down to the wood blocks. Pack modeling clay around the form (see photo 29). Then place the packed frame on a

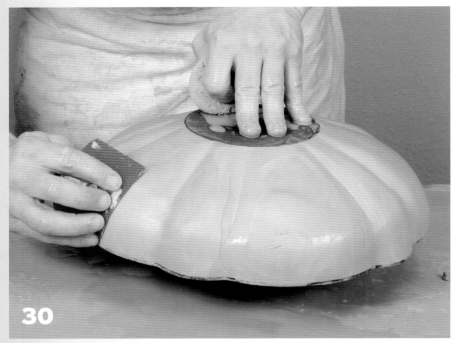

30

Modeling the body with a cheese cutter and ribs

piece of plaster or a *banding wheel* (a turntable for pottery) so that you can reach all portions of the exterior as you shape the clay. Model the body with a cheese cutter and ribs (see photo 30).

Cover the foot-interface template with a thick slab of clay (see photo 31). Then level the clay with cutting blocks and a wire. To create the profile of the foot, flip the foot template and clay onto a board and use a needle tool to cut the clay around the template (see photo 32).

Repeat these steps to make the foot and body prototypes for the second bowl. When you've finished modeling, place the foot prototypes on the body prototypes and check the proportions and relationship of the feet and bowl forms to each other (see photo 33).

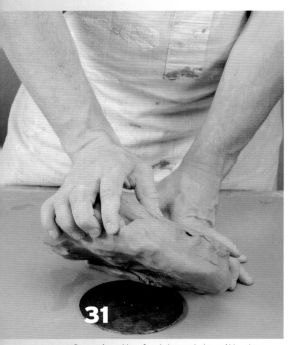

31

Covering the foot template with clay

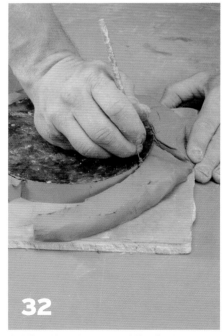

32

Cutting the clay around the foot template with a needle tool

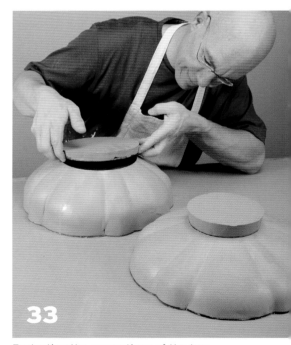

33

Evaluating the proportions of the two bowls

34

Sponging residual clay off the templates

Sponge any clay residue off the templates (see photo 34). In these two examples, you'll notice that the foot for the shallow bowl is both smaller in diameter and taller; the taller bowl has a wider, shorter foot. Remember that the foot and body parts will be cast separately and assembled after casting, so the prototypes can't include any undercuts. If you want the form of the body to expand beyond the diameter of the rim template and then come back in before meeting the foot, you'll need to make a two-piece mold for the body.

making the molds

Smooth the forms with a soft brush and water, then cast the two molds. The bodies are cast upside down, and the feet are cast right side up. To save plaster, place the bodies on plywood circles and build low walls of flashing around them (see photo 35). Pour

Steven Thurston

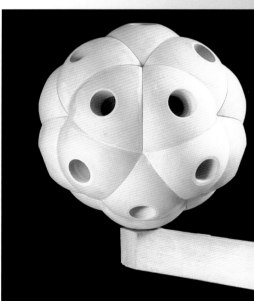

Composition No. 6 Equality, 2000
72 x 28 x 74 inches (182.9 x 71.1 x 188 cm)
Mold cast; mixed media
Photo by artist

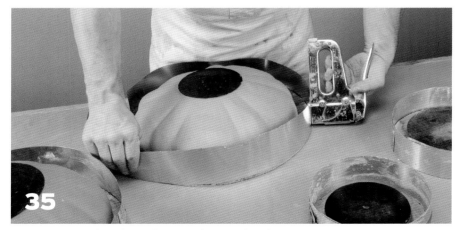

35

Assembling the flashing before pouring and frosting

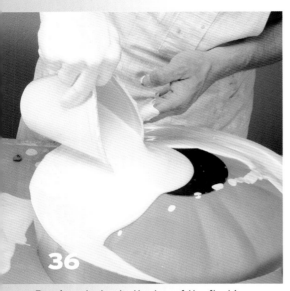

36

Pouring plaster to the top of the flashing

37

Frosting the plaster above the flashing

38

Leveling the bottom of the mold

enough plaster into the flashing to cover the upper section of each bowl (see photo 36). Then frost the remainder (see photo 37). Clean up the excess plaster and level the plaster while it's still soft (see photo 38). Cast each foot in a simple poured mold.

When the plaster has set, remove the templates (see photo 39). Then remove the prototypes (see photo 40). See pages 140–142 for instructions on attaching cast forms.

Rain Harris

Heirloom, 2005
12 x 13 x 8 inches (30.5 x 33 x 20.3 cm)
Slip-cast and assembled porcelain; cone 6;
luster and beads
Photo by John Carland

39

Removing the rim template

40

Checking the two molds

Andrew Martin

Tehran Splendor, 2006
4 x 12 ½ x 12 ½ inches (10.2 x 31.8 x 31.8 cm)
Slip-cast porcelain; electric fired, cone 7
Photo by Nick Elias

Andrew Martin

Baghdad Cafe–In Better Times, 2006
3 ½ x 6 x 6 inches (8.9 x 15.2 x 15.2 cm)
Slip-cast porcelain; electric fired, cone 7
Photo by Nick Elias

41

The finished cup and saucer prototypes

42

Making the cup and saucer molds

43

Removing the cup prototype

making cups & saucers

Cups and saucers are very easy forms to make, but achieving the right proportional relationship between them can be difficult. Making a cup that is easy and comfortable to pick up, that meets and leaves the lips gracefully, and that has a good weight-to-mass ratio—and a saucer that holds a spoon and a cookie—is a quintessential pleasure of mastery! There are a number of ways to approach the play of cup, saucer, hand, mouth, and hot liquid.

The cup and saucer shown in photo 41 are made in the same way as the footed bowls described on pages 45–49. The prototypes for the cup and its foot, for example, are designed with three templates. The one-piece mold for the cup's body and the one-piece mold for its foot are then cast separately, and the castings are attached to one another. The saucer is essentially a small, footed plate and is designed in the same way as the cup. (Handles are covered on pages 59–63.)

When I made my first saucer, the real challenge was how to create the saucer footwell for the cup. As I mulled this over, it suddenly became clear: a footwell in a saucer is an indentation in slip. All I needed to do was make a footwell in a small plate, and the plate would become a saucer! To make this footwell, I would cast a positive plaster form that I could use to make an indentation in the saucer.

When you're designing cups and saucers, begin by making paper cutouts of their rims and feet. Choose one cutout for each shape. Then make photocopies of the selected shapes in many sizes so that you can play with the proportions of the cup and saucer as part of the design process. This will help you to get a visual feeling for the volumes and relationships of the forms. You can also draw profiles to aid in the visualization.

Next, create the prototypes for the cup and saucer, using three templates for each. Then make the four molds: two for the bodies and two for the feet of your saucer and cup (see photo 42). When the plaster has set, remove the prototypes from the molds (see photo 43).

creating a footwell

Now you need to determine the size of the saucer footwell, which should be slightly larger than the foot of the cup but smaller than the foot of the saucer. From the paper cutouts you made earlier, choose one that is between those two sizes and place it in the saucer mold, under the template for the foot of the cup, to check its size (see photo 44). Cut this shape out from hardboard and use it to model a footwell prototype with nearly straight sides (see photo 45). Add a tapered square of clay to the top of this prototype to serve as a handle (see photo 46).

making the mold

Make a mold of the footwell prototype (see photo 47). When the plaster has set, remove the template and clean up the mold. Soap the mold and fill it with plaster. Then scrape and level the plaster to the top of the mold (see photo 48). The original mold is a waste mold; you'll have to destroy it in order to remove the straight-sided footwell form. When the plaster has set, make cuts in the waste mold and pry it off with a chisel (see photo 49). Clean and dry the plaster footwell form (see page 19). If you want to make multiples for production, cast a rubber master mold of this form (see pages 109–111). To use the plaster footwell form, refer to the instructions on page 136.

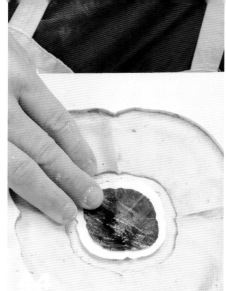

Using a cutout to determine the size of the footwell

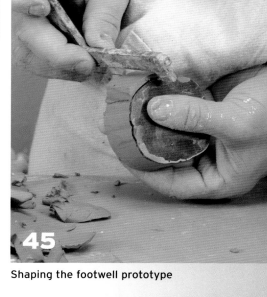

Shaping the footwell prototype

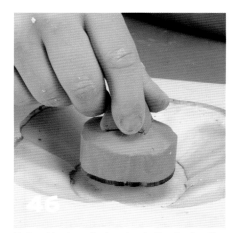

Using the handle to check the footwell prototype in the saucer

Pouring the footwell waste mold

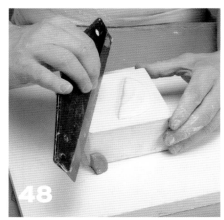

Scraping the excess plaster from the footwell waste mold

Removing the footwell mold from the waste mold

USING A WHEEL-THROWN RING TO MAKE A PLASTER PROTOTYPE

A quick way to generate many proto-types for bowls and plates is to throw 1-inch-thick (2.5 cm) clay rings without bottoms and alter them to the desired proportions and shapes (see photo 50). Let the clay stiffen to near *leather hard* (partly dry and stiff), then fill the ring to the top with plaster (see photo 51). When the plaster has set, remove the clay from around the plaster prototype (see photo 52). Alter the prototype if necessary, or just sand it to remove imperfections.

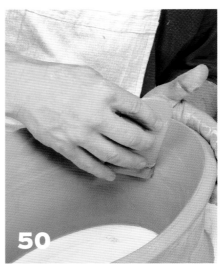

50

Smoothing the altered shape with a rib

Sanam Emami

***Trivet,* 2005**
1 x 8 x 8 inches (2.5 x 20.3 x 20.3 cm)
Slip-cast porcelain; stamped impressions, silk-screened underglaze; salt fired, cone 10
Photo by artist

51

Filling the ring with plaster

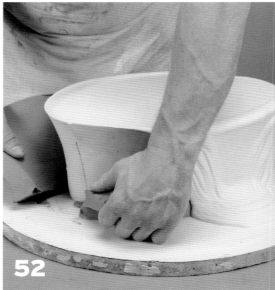

52

Removing the clay ring from the plaster prototype

Andrew Martin

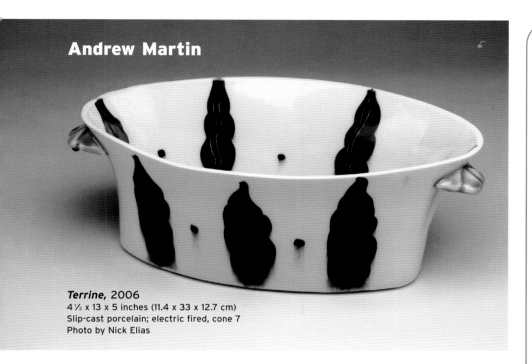

Terrine, 2006
4 ½ x 13 x 5 inches (11.4 x 33 x 12.7 cm)
Slip-cast porcelain; electric fired, cone 7
Photo by Nick Elias

making the mold

Place the prototype on a piece of plywood and staple flashing around the plywood edges. Soap the prototype, apply spray mold release to it, and pour the plaster. When the plaster has set, turn the mold on its side, tap around its perimeter to loosen the plaster prototype, and remove the prototype from the mold (see photos 53 and 54).

53

Loosening the prototype from the mold with a rubber mallet

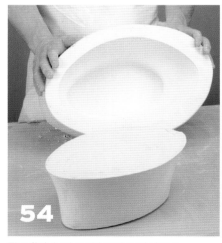

54

The finished mold and prototype

Chris Gustin

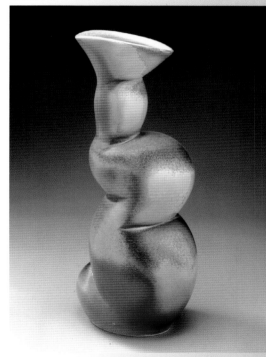

Alcobaca Vase #9910, 1999
22 x 8 x 8 inches (55.9 x 20.3 x 20.3 cm)
Slip-cast porcelain; wood fired in anagama kiln, cone 11
Photo by Dean Powell

56

Assembling the cottles around the prototype

CARVING A PLASTER PROTOTYPE FOR A ONE-PIECE MOLD

Prototypes can also be carved from plaster (see photo 55). I sometimes make prototypes for tumblers this way.

55

Carving a plaster prototype with a shaver

First I determine the height and rough diameter of each tumbler and pour a block of plaster from which I can make four prototypes. For a 7-inch-tall (17.8 cm) tumbler, 3 inches (7.6 cm) in diameter, I make a 3½ x 7 x 14-inch (8.9 x 17.8 x 35.6 cm) plaster block, then use a bow saw to cut this block into smaller ones. I carve each smaller block with a very sharp wood chisel or shave it with Surform tools. Then I use wet/dry sandpaper to finish it (see photo 55).

making the mold

To make the mold, soap one of the prototypes, invert it inside cottle boards, and cover it with plaster (see photos 56 and 57). Remove the prototype from the mold by placing it horizontally on the table and tapping its top with a rubber mallet to jar the prototype loose (see photo 58).

57

Pouring the plaster around the tumbler prototype

58

Tapping the mold to remove the prototype

Andrew Martin

Trichroma Tums, 2006
6 x 3 x 3 inches (15.2 x 7.6 x 7.6 cm)
Slip-cast porcelain; electric fired, cone 7
Photo by Nick Elias

Tom Spleth
cups and only cups

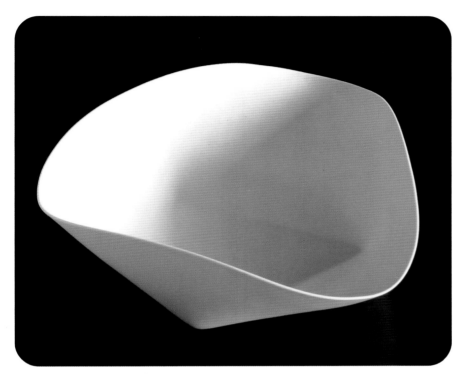

Black Sumi Drawing on Cup, 2006
3 x 3 x 3 ½ inches (7.6 x 7.6 x 8.9 cm)
Slip cast; unglazed porcelain, oxides
Photo by artist

When he finished graduate school in 1970, Tom Spleth elected to earn his living by making ceramics in a studio situation. Through what he describes as an unarticulated, intuitive leap, almost from the moment he started to produce work in his new studio, he began to experiment with slip casting, which at that time was considered to be an industrial process and, at best, only ancillary to good studio pottery practice. Tom feels that his key contribution to the art and craft of clay working then was to make slip casting the central idea for an individual who works alone.

Skeptical of the overwrought slip-cast products of industry, Tom devised methods of working with plaster that enabled him to bypass tradition-bound industrial procedures and work more directly with the materials. One of his early strategies was to make molds without models by cutting cast plaster into blocks and sheets with chisels and saws. This approach enabled Tom to create cast objects that retained their sense of gesture and revealed evidence of the maker's hand.

Tom refused to accept what he saw as the restrictive industrial forming

methods that were then the norm. As well as making molds without models, he developed an approach that involved pouring freshly mixed, fluid plaster onto tabletops and the floor, and then troweling forms into existence as the plaster set up. This method, he notes, requires athletic attention to the plaster, which changes its properties of strength and responsiveness over periods of time as short as five or 10 minutes. To use this method, he says, one's intent must be clear at the start. Even though the pieces that Tom made this way were the products of industrial plaster and fine-grained casting slip, the techniques that he used enabled him to create work that retained a distinct sense of the presence of an individual's hand.

Over the course of his long involvement with plaster and slip casting, Tom has also used conventional mold-making methods to produce forms that are more or less utilitarian, but these forms always provide a pristine, neutral ground for his drawing. For Tom, slip casting provides a ceramic surface comparable to a sheet of paper, upon which his drawings may appear.

Tom has made slip-cast cups for more than 30 years, which is a long time to spend on what, at first, may appear to be very simple objects. The cup continues to be engaging to him, however, and lately is practically all that he makes when he slip casts.

Tom describes the cup as a very intimate tool for conducting the necessary daily act of drinking. "The cup relates exactly to its user's hand and

"The cup reveals the depth of its character and how it relates to its user's life only after a long association."

mouth; the subtle amalgamation of its form and function must be right." It is also, in his view, a "short form," much like a song or haiku. The cup strikes Tom as having an inexhaustible capacity for conveying insight and expression, and for communication. In his travels near the Blue Ridge Mountains of his North Carolina home, Tom has seen cups "as light and delicate, yet as conflicted and presumptuous as the teatime cups served to old ladies on the verandas of ruined southern plantation homes." Other cups, he says, are as tough and industrial as they need to be in a corporate workplace, "where heads roll when plans fail."

Tom explains that the cup as a work of art is never relegated to the pedestal for long. Instead, as one grasps an actual cup and feels the warming of its cool ceramic texture, its mythical, timeless containership comes to the fore. "The cup reveals the depth of its character and how it relates to its user's life only after a long association."

Tom draws on some of his cups. These drawings, which are cobalt or iron inlaid into the body and covered by a clear glaze, are concentrated, cup-sized images that he adds to the surface with the cup's ritual of function in mind. Tom states that these images "may inform or expand the moment of use, may contrast with what is ordinarily a neutral act, or may serve to commiserate with the user." On some of Tom's cups, a few words appear on the surface. These "connect the user to everyday impertinences and thereby moderate the lofty idealism of the plain cup." For those who like a little less backtalk from their tableware, a few simple, unmarked cups are always available.

Tom aspires to exhibit the qualities of a cup himself; he says he'd like to be as straightforward, unassuming,

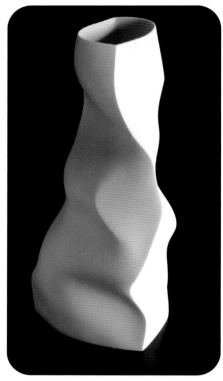

Carved Vase Form, 2005
7 x 6 x 15½ inches (17.8 x 15.2 x 39.4 cm)
Slip-cast porcelain; polished, unglazed porcelain
Photo by artist

transparent, and generous in his daily practice. Everything he has learned, Tom says, both within the studio and in the world, appears implicitly in the cups that he creates. Occasionally, he also aspires to make a decent cup, thereby ensuring himself "an association with the cup-as-teacher."

As life unfolds on a planet filled with atrocity, Tom feels that the cup embodies a concept of peace and its attendant rituals, however ordinary those rituals may seem. "The big headline ideas, fueled by greed, violence, and the desire for power, seem to override the cup's gentle consecrations. Be that as it may, the cup always makes a quiet request for kindness: 'Hear, pause, and receive.'"

Don't Harsh My Buzz, 2006
3 x 3 x 3½ inches (7.6 x 7.6 x 8.9 cm)
Slip-cast porcelain; underglaze decoration, clear glaze
Photo by artist

Tom believes that the slip caster answers to two masters: the craft of working with cool plaster to make intricate molds, and the completely separate discipline of ceramics and fire. "Artists who pursue mold making must have, in addition to all the skills that go into producing ceramics, an aptitude for mechanical assembly and thinking in reverse three-dimensionality."

When a freshly slip-cast clay form is first removed from its mold, it strikes Tom as perfect—in his words, "strangely passive, seismically delicate, receptive, damp, and tender." Its maker's slightest touch, he says, introduces asymmetry to the impressionable clay object, which has an exact memory for such things. Later the heat of the kiln warps the cup even more, drawing it nearer to what Tom feels is the profound perfection of ceramics. He most loves cups that have been randomly moved by the fire.

In his workshop, the adjustments Tom makes to the chemistry of his ware are, for him, as much a part of the creative process as sculpting a form. "The aesthetics of the work and its chemical formulae develop incrementally, in small steps, hand in hand, over many years." His cups, for example, started with his ideas about the sensuality of matte surfaces but moved on when he realized that a gloss glaze is actually more sensual. Tom sees the gloss surfaces of his cups as metaphorically wet, not dry, and he points out that the watery gloss responds magically to light due to the ever-changing reflections on it and to the microscopic bubbles that fill the body of the glaze. The surfaces of his cups, he believes, engender more confidence in the user because their gloss invites touch, as

Bowl with Checkerboard Exterior, 2000
8 x 7 x 3½ inches (20.3 x 17.8 x 8.9 cm)
Slip cast; underglaze decoration, clear glaze
Photo by artist

TOM SPLETH received his B.F.A. from the Kansas City Art Institute and his M.F.A. from the New York State College of Ceramics at Alfred University, where he later taught. His work has since been featured, along with that of 17 former faculty members, in the Schein-Joseph International Museum of Ceramic Art at Alfred and in permanent collections at the Rhode Island School of Design, the Corning Museum of Glass in New York, and the University of Illinois at Urbana-Champaign.

Tom has been an artist-in-residence at the John Michael Kohler Arts Center in Wisconsin. His work been reviewed by several well-known ceramic periodicals, including *Clay Art* and *Studio Potter*. He currently lives in North Carolina, where he teaches at Penland School of Crafts and Odyssey Center for the Ceramic Arts. The natural environment and forest surrounding his home are often reflected in his ceramic objects.

well as sending the message that the cups are impervious and easy to clean. These qualities register with the user instantaneously, nonverbally, and subliminally, and the psychological moment when that happens, he feels, is the work's tipping point—the point at which the cups flow away from the studio into the lives of others.

multiple-piece molds

Molds of two or more pieces are used for forms that have undercuts or complexities that can't be accommodated by a one-piece mold. If an undercut is small and will make no difference to the overall effect of the form, filling the undercut and making a simpler mold is preferable; you can carve the undercut back into the pot after the pot is cast. But if your form has a large undercut that is integral to it, you'll have to design the mold to accommodate this undercut by adding one or more extra mold sections. Some forms that require two-piece molds include handles, spouts, spherical forms, tiles, pitchers, and complex vases.

MAKING TWO-PIECE MOLDS

There are only a few ways to split a mold into two pieces—usually vertically or horizontally. In the pitcher mold described on pages 65–67, for example, I've placed the vertical seam on the ends of the pitcher and the horizontal seam on the bottom corner, where the floor meets the wall. Locating the seam here instead of on the bottom eliminates the seam mark and also makes it very easy to clean up the cast piece for bisque firing.

Seams running across the bottom of a casting will always show after firing, even if they've been well scraped and sponged. To avoid this problem, locate the seams on corners or curves so that you can remove them easily from the *green ware* (clay that has been dried and is ready to fire).

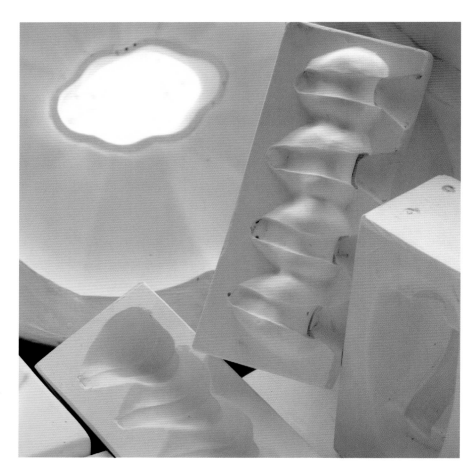

If your form is spherical, you can divide it horizontally across its widest part. A good example of this is the cap-lid jar described on pages 82–87. The bottom of the mold for this jar creates the floor and lower wall up to the jar's widest point, and the upper section creates the upper portion of the jar, from its widest cross-section to the top of the *flange.* (The flange is the portion of a casting that ensures registration of a body and lid.)

making handles

With practice, using a two-piece mold to make a handle is very easy. I make three basic types of slip-cast handles. One looks like a pulled strap, one looks like a coil, and the third is sculpted to look like a shell. I use plastilene to make the prototypes for all three.

In the examples that follow, we'll make all three types of handles. All of them can be either drain cast or solid cast; the size and mass of the handle prototype will determine which method you employ. If the handle is more than ⅝-inch (1.6 cm) thick, design the mold to be drain cast. If it's thinner, it can be cast solid.

Drain-cast molds must be designed to provide two openings: one that serves as an entrance and exit for the slip, and one that will allow air to enter and exit. A solid-cast mold requires only one opening because the slip goes in but never comes out. In the examples that follow, the strap handle and the sculpted shell handle are both solid cast; the mold for each has only one opening. The coil handle, which is drain cast, has two. Drain-cast handle molds make it possible to create massive handles that are very light because they're hollow.

The most forgiving material from which to make a handle prototype is plastilene. The firmest varieties are the best; they can take a lot of abuse during the molding process and still yield excellent results.

To make either a strap or coil handle, start by working the plastilene in your hands to soften it to a malleable condition. You can also leave it in the sun or in a warm (not hot) location; it's easier to work into a homogeneous mass when it's warm. Make a thick coil, then roll it thinner where you want the handle to bend, and leave it thicker at the ends, where it will attach to the pot. Practice a few times to get the feel of the technique. Now shape the coil. If you want to make a strap-type handle, flatten the coil with the outer edge of your hand, bend it to the shape that you want, and cut off

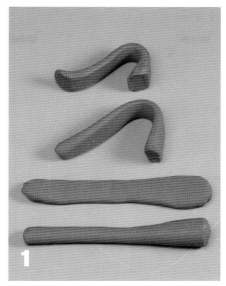

The stages of making a strap handle

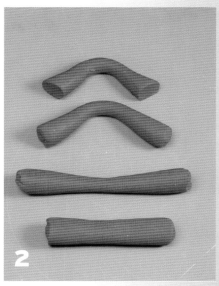

The stages of making a coil handle

the excess (see photo 1). For a coil-type handle, leave the coil rounded (see photo 2).

Next, check to see if the proportion of the rough handle fits well with the body prototype. Using a long craft blade or a sharp fettling knife, cut the angle and curves of the handle and test-fit it to the body prototype. The

handle prototype won't stick to wet clay, so pin it to the body with a needle tool. (The mark left on the body by the needle tool will help you position the cast handle correctly when you attach it to the cast body.) Once you've achieved the desired proportion, place the handle prototype in the refrigerator or freezer to stiffen it up for molding.

removing prototypes from molds

When you use clay prototypes to make multiple-piece molds, don't remove the prototype until the mold is completely finished. Removing clay prototypes distorts them; they won't fit back into the mold exactly. This will result in mold seams that don't fit exactly. I usually use wet clay prototypes, but if your clay prototype is bone dry (so that you can carve fine details in it, for example), make all the mold sections, in quick succession, in one day. If a dry clay prototype sits in wet plaster overnight or even for several hours, it will begin to rehydrate and swell. The prototype will swell out of the first mold section; it will be distorted and will distort the finished casting, as well.

Removing plaster prototypes is often quite easy. Simply clean up the mold and place the plaster back in it before casting the next section. When using plastilene, don't remove it from the mold during casting; it will warp, just as plastic clay will.

Lesley Baker

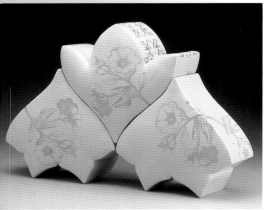

Elements, 2005
30 x 40 x 10 inches (76.2 x 101.6 x 25.4 cm)
Slip-cast vitreous china; silk-screened underglaze
and laser decals, cone 10
Photo by artist

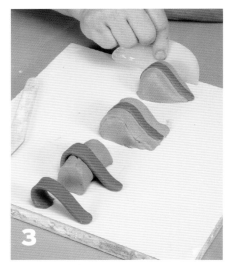

The stages of blocking in a strap handle

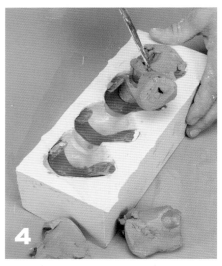

Removing the blocking clay from the
first mold section

solid-cast strap handles

When the prototype is firm, fit it around a very soft mound of plastic clay and fit thin slabs up to and perpendicular to the widest part of the edge of the handle. The goal here is to have the two parts of the mold meet squarely at the handle's long edges. A thin edge on one side of the mold will tend to chip, creating more work during cleanup of the green ware. Now that you've blocked in the prototype, use a fettling knife to cut away the excess plastic clay that supports it, shaping the clay mound at an angle to eliminate any undercuts (see photo 3).

The inner surface of a strap-handle prototype may curl in on itself, creating an undercut, but the outer surface must have no undercuts. After the handle is cast, you simply remove the flexible prototype from the mold. If a strap handle loops back on itself very severely, there are two ways to approach designing the mold. One method is to straighten out the handle prototype slightly before you mold it

and then re-form the handle after it is cast in clay but before it has hardened. The other approach is to divide the handle down its central axis rather than along its edges, and split the mold side to side. To do this, you'll position the prototype on one edge and bury it halfway in blocking clay before pouring the first mold section.

Once the prototype is blocked in plastic clay, position cottles around it, leaving about 1 inch (2.5 cm) between the mound and each cottle. Cover the mound and prototype with plaster. When the plaster has set, disassemble the cottles and lift or slide this mold section off the work surface. Place the mold in a sink or bucket filled with cold water and soak it for about 15 minutes. The heat of the plaster will have softened the plastilene, so the prototype will be very soft; placing the mold in cold water will both stiffen the prototype and soften the plastic blocking clay. Because the plaster has set and the prototype is oil based, you don't need

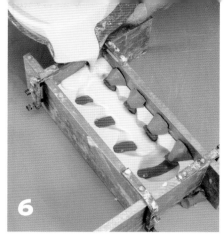

6

Pouring the second mold section

5

Attaching the clay pour-spout prototype

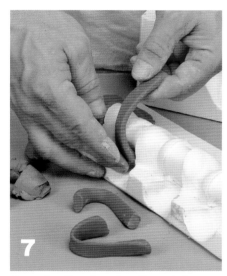

7

Removing the strap-handle prototype

to worry about water damaging the mold or the prototype.

Remove the blocking clay with a fettling knife (see photo 4). To remove any additional blocking clay that remains around the prototype, loosen it with a soft-bristle brush. Check to make sure that the mound of clay you just removed has left no undercuts. Carefully sand the plaster to remove any undercuts and any roughness, taking care not to damage the prototype. If the prototype comes out of the mold, don't worry. Just clean all the blocking clay from it, soap the mold, and reinsert the prototype into the mold.

As I noted earlier, a thin strap handle can be solid cast, so the mold will require only one hole. To create this pour hole, first make a small cone out of blocking clay. Then remove the tip of this model, cut it into a half-cone shape, and position it on the mold, with its cutoff tip resting on the thickest part of the handle prototype, usually at the handle's thick end (see

photo 5). Make sure the tip of the cone is both wide and thick; this will prevent the pour hole in the finished mold from clogging with slip before the handle is fully cast. (After the mold is cast, you can enlarge the resulting pour hole with a knife or chisel.)

Now soap the mold, apply spray mold release, and pour plaster on top of the first section, making sure that it's about 1½ inches (3.8 cm) thick (see photo 6). No keys are necessary because the mound of blocking clay acted as one huge key model. When the plaster is cured, remove the cottles, separate the mold sections, and remove the handle prototype (see photo 7).

Mathew S. McConnell

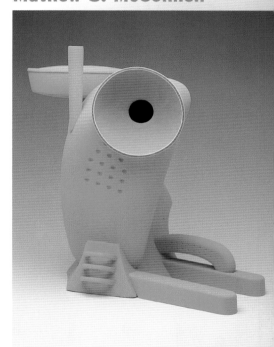

EASX050L1105A14, 2005
14 x 8 x 6 inches (35.6 x 20.3 x 15.2 cm)
Slip-cast and assembled earthenware; cone 05
Photo by artist

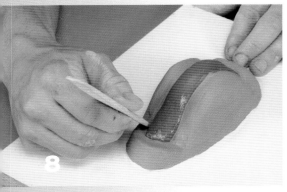

8

Blocking in the coil-handle prototype

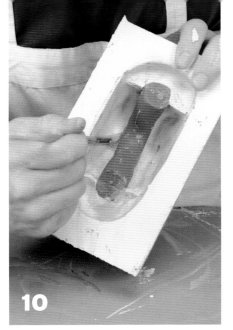

10

Brushing residual clay from the mold and prototype

11

Pinning clay-filled plastic tubes to the prototype

9

Removing the blocking clay

drain-cast coil handles

In this example, the handle, which I cast for an overhang lid (see pages 77–81), is drain cast rather than solid cast, so you'll need to add a fill hole at each end of the mold. (Remember, small handles can be solid cast; large ones should be drain cast.)

Begin making the mold by first blocking in the handle prototype, making sure that the blocking clay divides the handle at its widest point and also covers the area that will attach to the lid (see photo 8). Pour the first mold sec-

tion. When the plaster is set, put the mold and the clay in cold water. This will soften the blocking clay and will also firm up the prototype, which will have been softened by the heat of the plaster as it set. When the blocking clay has softened, remove it with a fettling knife (see photo 9). Using running water and a soft bristle brush, clean out any blocking clay that is stuck to the prototype (see photo 10). Sand away any roughness or undercuts from the recess left by the mound of clay.

Soap the mold and apply spray mold release. Center a plastic tube at each end of the prototype, where the handle will be attached to the pot. Pack the two tubes with soft clay so they don't fill up with plaster, and pin them to the prototype with needle tools (see photo 11). Soap the plaster and apply spray mold release to the first mold section. Finally, pour the plaster to fill the underside of the handle.

When you pour the slip during casting, you'll pour it into funnels placed in the plastic tubes. Because the plastic won't absorb water from the slip, the holes

12

Removing the prototype from the coil-handle mold

will remain open during casting. After the plaster is set, separate the mold and remove the prototype (see photo 12).

solid-cast shell handles

The prototypes for these are simply sculpted out of plastilene. Begin by rolling out a coil of clay, tapering the ends as you do. Pound the coil with the soft edge of your hand to flatten it somewhat. Fit the handle to the piece you are making to check the proportional relationship. When the handle fits, finish sculpting the detail into the form (see photo 13).

Next, bury the prototype halfway in blocking clay so that the seam line will be at the edge of the handle (see photo 14). Pour the plaster. When it has set, remove the blocking clay, cut keys, sand away any roughness, soap this mold section well, and apply spray mold release. Just as you did with the strap handle, add a half-cone shape with its tip cut off, placing it on the prototype where the handle will attach to the pot (see photo 15). Then pour the second mold section. When the plaster has set, remove the prototypes (see photo 16).

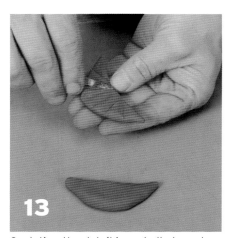

13

Sculpting the detail in a shell-shaped handle

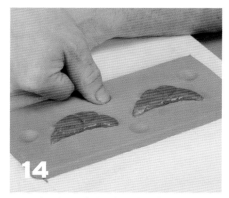

14

Pressing keys into the blocking clay

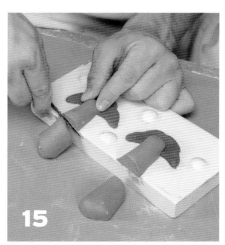

15

Fitting the pour-hole prototypes to the spouts

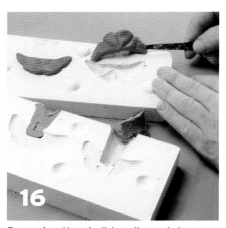

16

Removing the shell-handle prototypes

Richard Shaw

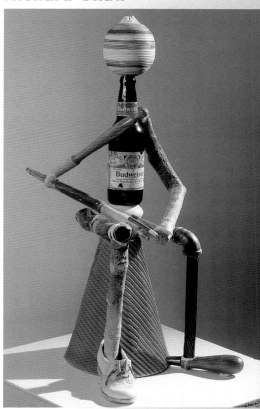

Seated Figure with Beer Bottle, 2005
25 x 16 x 11 inches (63.5 x 40.6 x 27.9 cm)
Slip-cast porcelain; glaze, cone 6; overglaze, cone 018; decals
Photo by Schopplein Studios

making spouts

Industrial prototypes, including those for spouts, are traditionally made of plaster, and this is what is often recommended to mold-making students. I've also seen potters make spout prototypes by pulling porcelain clay as if they were making handles, and then bisque firing the prototypes before making the molds. Either of these methods will work, but I prefer the easiest solution—making spout prototypes from plastilene.

Warm the plastilene to working condition and roll it into a tapered coil that's approximately the right size for your spout. Bend the coil and cut it into the desired spout shape and length (see photo 17). Often I have to make several prototypes before I create the one that has the best relationship to the pot.

Once you're satisfied with the proportion, test-fit the prototype to the body. Make a mark on the body prototype with a needle tool so you can attach the cast spout to the same spot.

Sometimes a variety of different spouts—and two or three different handles—will work on the same teapot body. Don't hesitate to make prototypes and molds for all the handle and spout forms you like. The finished molds will allow you to create a variety of different teapots from the same body mold.

To cast the spout mold, bury the prototype halfway down in a slab of blocking clay, leaving 1¼ inches (3.2 cm) of space between the prototype and the cottle boards. Create keys by making indentations in the blocking clay. Place a large, half-cone-shaped piece of clay, with its tip cut off, on the attachment area of the spout (see photo 18). This will form the basic pour hole that will allow the slip to enter and exit the mold. (You can enlarge the hole in the mold later if necessary.) Pour the plaster and, when it has set, pull off the blocking clay and use a soft brush and water to remove the bits of clay stuck to the plaster and prototype.

Use medium- and then fine-grit wet/dry sandpaper to sand the plaster where the two parts of the mold will meet. Attach the second half of the pour spout to the prototype and smooth the clay with a sponge (see photo 19). Soap this mold section well, apply spray mold release, and pour the second mold section. Don't worry about the tip of the spout being closed when you cast it. You'll cut it open with a craft knife after you attach the cast spout to the pot. Clean the finished mold with vinegar (see photo 20). Use 600-grit wet/dry sandpaper to remove any roughness in the casting surface, but be careful not to sand any areas where the mold sections will meet.

Bending the spout to the desired shape

Cleaning up the clay where the pour-hole and spout prototypes meet

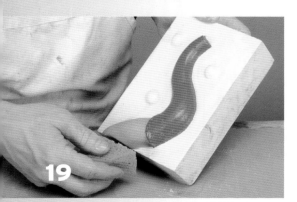

Cleaning up the second section of the pour-hole prototype

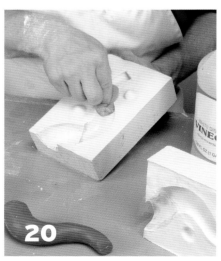

Cleaning the mold with vinegar

21

Modeling the prototype by hand

making pitchers

The pitcher prototype in this example was modeled in clay without using templates (see photo 21). Model a handle prototype from plastilene; you'll attach the cast handle to the body casting later (see photo 22). Pitchers and gravy boats are only slightly different from vases and tumblers, which can also be made with two-piece molds that split vertically. The one difference is that the rim of the pitcher form is usually curved. Adding a thick slab of clay to the top of the form will create a reservoir and level the top of the mold (see photo 23). After you cast the form, you'll cut off this excess clay with a craft knife.

Vladimir Groh & Yasuyo Nishida

Hotaru Rabbit Cup, 2006
5 x 5 x 3 inches (12.7 x 12.7 x 7.6 cm)
Cast porcelain; gas fired, patina overglaze
Photo by Vladimir Groh

22

Checking the handle prototype against the body form

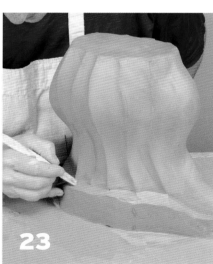

23

Shaping a reservoir for a contoured rim

Linda Cordell

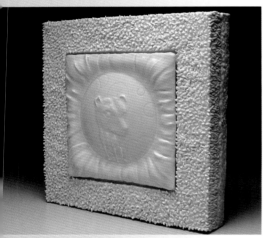

Memento, 2005
12 x 12 x 3 inches (30.5 x 30.5 x 7.6 cm)
Modeled, carved, cast, and altered porcelain; clear
glaze; cone 10
Photo by artist

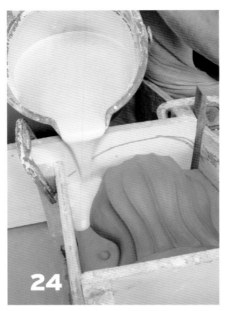

24

Pouring the plaster for the first mold
section

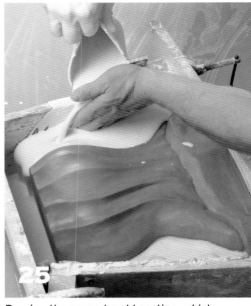

25

Pouring the second mold section, which
includes the floor

26

Checking the thickness of the frosted
belly area

27

Cutting excess plaster off the mold

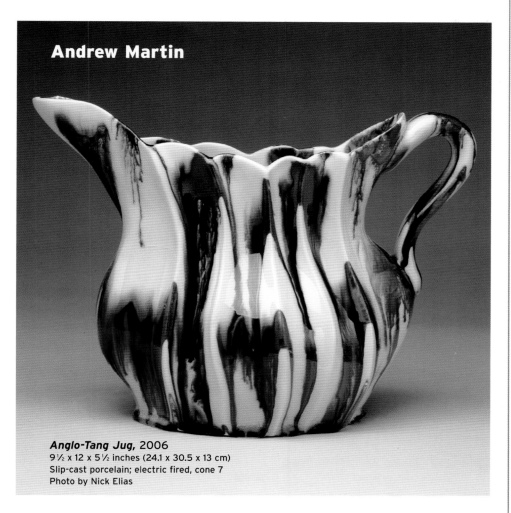

Andrew Martin

Anglo-Tang Jug, 2006
9 ½ x 12 x 5 ½ inches (24.1 x 30.5 x 13 cm)
Slip-cast porcelain; electric fired, cone 7
Photo by Nick Elias

Amy Lenharth

Pod Form, 2006
3 ½ x 4 x 6 inches (8.9 x 10.2 x 15.2 cm)
Slip-cast porcelain; terra sig and glaze;
cone 10, reduction; luster, cone 018
Photo by Janet Ryan

To make the mold, first bury the body prototype halfway in clay, on its side, and assemble the cottle boards, using them to block off the top and bottom of the prototype. Pour the plaster over the first side (see photo 24). After the plaster has set and you've cleaned it up for the second pour, cut keys. Apply mold soap and spray mold release to the plaster. Then pour the second mold section, which will form the second side and the floor of the pitcher (see photo 25). I frosted this mold at the belly to make sure it was thick enough and checked the thickness with one finger (see photo 26).

When the plaster has set, open the mold and remove the prototype. In this example, I let the plaster fill all the way to the table, so the second section has square corners. Using a bow saw, simply cut off the excess plaster (see photo 27).

making tiles

Slip-cast tiles are very easy to make and, unlike other types of tiles, will never warp during drying or firing because the slip-casting sedimentation process results in no tension in the aligned clay particles. When tiles are rolled from plastic clay, the possibility for warping is always present, although press-molded tiles may warp less than rolled ones.

The tile-making process requires some calculations. Knowing the maximum size that your kiln shelves will accommodate and the finished dimension of each tile, including its thickness, is important. The other factor to consider, of course, is your slip shrinkage (see pages 11–12).

Tile prototypes can be made in a number of different ways. You can use a clay slab, clear acrylic sheeting, or hardboard, or you can cast Hydrocal plaster prototypes. If you plan to produce numerous molds, a Hydrocal prototype is best because it's very hard and will better withstand the molding process. I never make more than a few tile molds, so rather than making a plaster master mold, I just reuse the prototype to make individual working molds for each tile.

To make a Hydrocal prototype, begin with four pieces of ¼- to ½-inch-square

(.6 to 1.3 cm) steel bar stock, which is available at well-stocked lumberyards. Select a width based on how thick you want your tiles to be, and have the bar stock cut longer than the largest tile you anticipate making. Usually 18 inches (45.7 cm) is long enough. While you're at the lumberyard, purchase a cut-in tool from the paint section. Painters use this tool when painting inside corners and edges; you'll use it to scrape excess plaster from your tile prototype and will find that it's handy for other studio tasks, too.

Refer to the shrinkage-calculation formula on page 12. If you're making a 10-inch-square (25.4 cm) tile from clay with a 12-percent shrinkage factor, the prototype should be approximately 11⅜ inches (29 cm) square. Use a marker to draw a line on each bar at 11⅜ inches (29 cm).

Next, you'll lay out the bars on a smooth surface, with the marks facing up, to form a plaster-retaining structure for pouring. Start by securing the first bar in place with blocking clay. Align the second bar with a carpenter's square to make sure it's perpendicular to the first, then secure it, too. Continue until all the bars are in place. To check that the bars form a perfect square, measure the square from one corner to the opposite corner. Then measure the distance between the

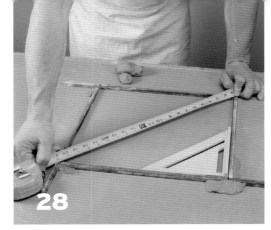

28

Checking the tile frame for square

other two corners. The two measurements should be exactly the same (see photo 28). Spray the interior of the frame you've created with spray mold release.

Mix the Hydrocal and pour it into the frame (see photo 29). Using the cut-in tool, scrape off the excess plaster during the plastic phase of the setting process (see photo 30). Then let the plaster prototype set until cured. When the Hydrocal is cured, it should release easily from the smooth work surface because the heat forces water between the mold and the work surface.

Before making the mold, you can finish the tile prototype edges in a variety of ways. For example, using a Surform planer to bevel each one by 5 degrees will ensure an easy release from the mold (see photo 31). If the tile will be a wall or floor tile, this bevel will also

Lesley Baker

Egg Flowers, 2005
8 x 18 x 4 inches (20.3 x 45.7 x 10.2 cm)
Slip-cast vitreous china; silk-screened underglaze and laser decals, cone 10
Photo by artist

29

Pouring the Hydrocal into the tile frame

30

Scraping the Hydrocal level with the frame

31

Beveling the edge of the tile prototype

help the grout hold the tile in place. Decide whether you want the tile edges to be sharp or rounded. If you want rounded edges, simply sand them with wet/dry sandpaper.

Soap the tile prototype, apply spray mold release to it, and lay it flat on the work surface, right side up, with the widest part (the back) on the table. Press a small coil of clay along its

edges, smoothing the clay to match the bevel on the prototype. This coil will keep the prototype from shifting as you make the mold and will account for any remaining undercuts. Assemble the cottles around the prototype and cover it with plaster. Once the plaster is cured, cut keys in it and apply mold soap and spray mold release to its bottom and edges. You may notice that the tile prototype is now loose in the mold. This is because the mold has expanded during the curing process. Don't worry about this.

The completed two-piece mold will need two fill tubes: one for filling it with slip and one to release air as the slip enters the mold. You'll set these plastic tubes in the plaster as you pour the next piece. The funnels that you use for casting must fit inside these tubes, so test-fit them before the next step. To prevent the plastic tubes from sliding out of the finished mold, cut each one to 1½ inches (3.8 cm) in length and wrap it with a narrow piece of duct tape. The tape will act as an undercut and will lock the tubes in place as the plaster sets around them.

Richard Swanson

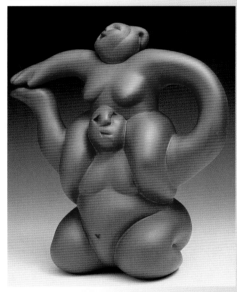

Sitting Pretty Teapot, 1993
9 x 7 ½ x 4 inches (22.9 x 19 x 10.2 cm)
Modeled, high-iron slip; electric fired, cone 5
Photo by artist

Ilena Finocchi

Harbingers, 2005
8 x 10 x 4 feet (2.4 x 3 x 1.2 m)
Black and white porcelain; electric fired,
cone 6
Photo by artist

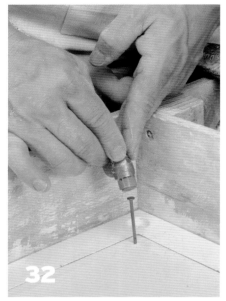

Placing the clay-filled tubes on the nails

Next, place two small finishing nails in opposite corners of the prototype, about ½ inch (1.3 cm) in from the edge. Fill the tubes with plastic clay and place them over the nails, with the nails inside the clay-filled tubes (see photo 32). The nails will hold the tubes in place while the plaster is poured around them. Now pour the second piece of the mold.

When the plaster has cured, disassemble the mold, remove the prototype, and clean and dry the mold. When slip casting this mold, use two C-clamps to hold the two sections together, tightening the clamps just enough to grip the sections firmly. Tightening the clamps too much can break the mold. If the mold is too thick for the clamps,

Andrew Martin

Ornament to "The Brightness", 1991
4 ½ x 12 x 12 inches (11.4 x 30.5 x 30.5 cm)
Slip-cast porcelain vase
Photo by Ron Johnson

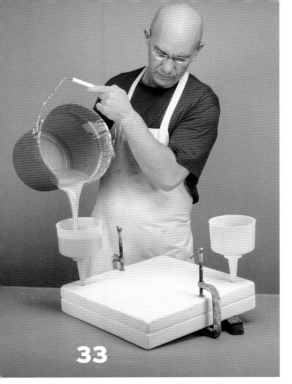

33

Pouring the slip into the mold

before you dry the mold, just cut away enough of the plaster to accommodate the clamps.

Before slip casting a tile, insert plastic funnels into the pour holes, then prop up one corner of the mold so that one funnel is slightly higher than the other. Pour the slip into the funnel that's lower (see photo 33). As the slip fills the mold from below, air will escape through the other funnel; eventually that funnel will begin to fill with slip.

making tile setters

As a pot shrinks during the firing, its outer edges will move inward toward the pot's center. To prevent the pot from moving on the kiln shelf as this shrinkage occurs, the pot is placed on a tile setter in the kiln (see photo below); the setter shrinks along with the pot. When certain pots, such as footed bowls, are fired without setters, they tend to warp and even crack. Setters are particularly helpful with these forms and with high-shrinkage clay bodies, which are especially likely to warp when placed directly on the kiln shelf. Firing in an electric kiln with high-sodium glazes poses another problem: even if an alumina kiln wash is used to protect the kiln shelves, the shelves become coated with residual sodium, and pots tend to fuse to them during firing.

To make tile setters, follow the same basic steps for making tiles. A hardboard or clear acrylic prototype will work fine because the setter tolerances need not be exact. (Remember to apply spray lubricant to hardboard in order to keep the plaster from sticking.) The setters can be as thin as $1/4$ inch (.6 cm) and require very little slip when cast. You can make a setter to fit a particular form, such as a large footed platter, or you can cut various shapes from a larger tile to fit the footprints of specific forms. (See page 143 for instructions on preparing tile setters for use.)

Placing a teacup on a tile setter

Richard Shaw

Sevrés Hat Jar, 1989
8 x 13 x 13 inches (20.3 x 33 x 33 cm)
Slip-cast porcelain; glaze, cone 10; underglaze, cone 18; decals
Photo by artist

Von Venhuizen

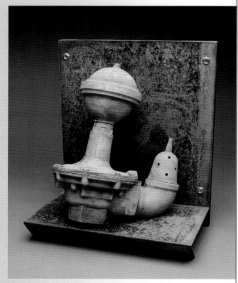

Recluse, 2004
15 x 12 x 8 inches (38.1 x 30.5 x 20.3 cm)
Slip-cast porcelain; gas fired, cone 10,
reduction; mixed media
Photo by artist

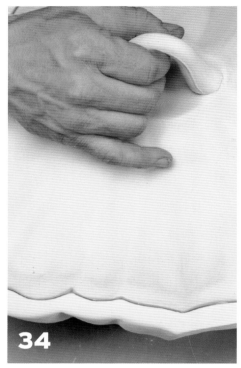

34

Notice the relationship between the lid
and flange.

making lidded forms

I've developed several methods to
ensure that a lid of any shape will fit
perfectly. It was here that my template
system really began to help me solve
technical problems related to form. In
this section you'll find instructions for
constructing an inset lid with the
flange on the body, an overhang lid
with the flange on the lid itself, and
cap lids of two different kinds—one
that meets the body rim to rim, and
one that sits on the shoulder of teapot
or jar forms.

The key to making any of these styles
of lids is the common element shared
between the lid and body. In the inset
lid example (see the next section), the
lid-and-flange template is the common
element. In the overhang lid (see pages
77–81), the common element is the
shape of the interior top portion of the
slip-cast body. A close fit is not good
enough. One look at poorly designed,
commercial slip-cast lids will illustrate
this clearly.

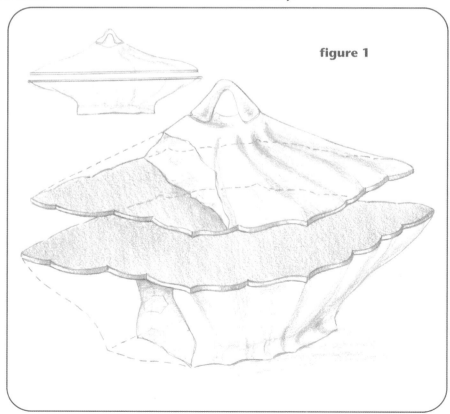

figure 1

inset lid

The first lid I made was an inset lid (see figure 1). For months I'd tried to figure out a way to make a lid of this type that would fit perfectly and work smoothly. Creating a common element (a flange) between the lid and the body turned out to be the key. I realized that the bottom of the lid and the upper surface of the flange had to be exactly the same. I solved this problem by using the same template to form the flange prototype and the lid prototype. The lid and the body flange work just like the ones shown in photo 34.

To make forms with inset lids, begin by drawing the shape of the body—at its rim—on paper. Cut out this shape and trace it onto another piece of paper. Inside this tracing, draw a lid-and-flange shape at least ¼ inch (.6 cm) smaller at its edge than the traced body-rim shape, and cut it out. To make the body-rim template, transfer the larger cutout to ⅛-inch-thick (.3 cm) hardboard and cut it out. Transfer the smaller lid-and-flange cutout to ¼-inch-thick (.6 cm) hardboard and cut this out, too. Before modeling the prototypes, place the smaller template on top of the larger one to check the clearance between what will be the lid and the rim of the body.

If you plan to cast a foot for the form (the example here doesn't have one), determine the shape of the footprint at this stage of the design process. Draw it on paper, transfer the shape to ⅛-inch-thick (.3 cm) hardboard, and cut out two identical templates for the floor of the form and the foot. Mark

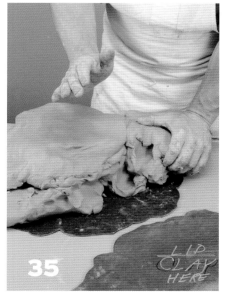

35

Packing clay on the body template

36

Modeling the body with a sponge

them "foot interface" and "body interface" (for a refresher, see pages 44–45).

To model the prototypes for the lid and body (and foot, if one is included), first pack clay on them and then shape

them (see photos 35 and 36). Also make the prototype for the handle. Test all the prototypes together to check their proportions and make adjustments when necessary (see photo 37). In this example, I altered the body further to make an implied foot.

37

Testing the handle on the prototype

Paul McMullan

Don't Park Here, 2005
22 x 15 x 8 inches (55.9 x 38.1 x 20.3 cm)
Slip cast, slab built; underglaze, cone 04;
glaze fired, oxidation
Photo by Jerry Mathieson

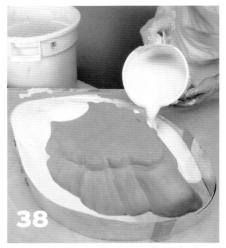

38

Pouring the lower portion of the body
mold before frosting the upper portion

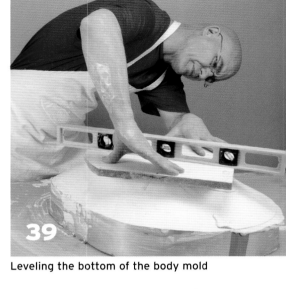

39

Leveling the bottom of the body mold

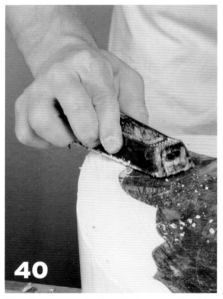

40

Shaving away plaster that ran under the
template

When the prototypes are finished,
make one-piece molds of each form
(see photo 38). If you frost the molds,
be sure to level their bottoms (see
photo 39). Avoid chipping the molds
by shaving off any plaster that has run
underneath the templates before

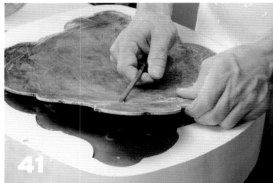

41

Removing the lid template for later use
in forming the flange

removing them (see photo 40). Be sure
to preserve the lid-and-flange template
because you'll use it to make the prototype for the flange (see photo 41).

Remove 1½ inches (3.8 cm) of clay
from around the edges of the body
prototype, then cut keys in the upper
edge of the mold (see photos 42 and
43). Apply the mold soap. Next, fill the
mold with soft modeling clay, leaving a
recess in the center but making sure
there's a solid layer of very soft clay
around the inner edges of the mold.

Removing clay in preparation for making the flange

Sanding the keys in the rim of the mold

Leveling the clay to the edge of the mold. (Notice the recess in the center of the soft clay.)

Remove the excess clay from above the edges of the mold and level the clay around them to conform to the top edge of the mold (see photo 44).

Drill four large holes in the lid-and-flange template to serve as finger grips when you create the flange prototype (see photo 45). Sponge the residual clay off the plaster, then dust the clay inside the mold, using a sock filled with nepheline syenite or Chinese dust (see page 139). Dusting the soft clay will prevent the template from sticking to it (see photo 46). Align the lid-and-flange template with the clay-filled body mold.

To form the flange prototype for the lid, first use a rubber mallet to pound the template into the clay until the top surface of the template is level with the top of the mold (see photo 47). Trim away any clay that's been displaced between the template and mold. You'll notice that the recess in the center will be filled in with clay displaced by the pressure of the template. If necessary, fill in any low areas around the lid-and-flange template with additional clay.

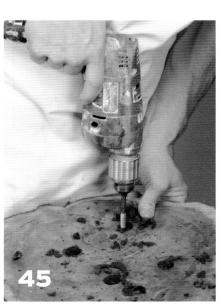

Drilling finger holes in the lid-and-flange template

Dusting the soft clay with Chinese dust

Pounding the template into the soft clay

75

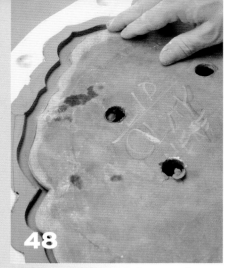

48

Removing the template from the formed flange

49

Adding a tapered block of clay for a pour hole

50

Lifting the flange mold, with the body prototype stuck to it

Now shift the template back and forth; doing this will give the cast lid some play (see photo 48). Your goal when fitting a lid is to allow enough play for the lid to be comfortably snug without being extremely tight. You'll need to consider the fact that plaster molds deteriorate over time. As they do, your inset lids will get larger and your body flanges smaller, so the lids will begin to fit tighter and tighter. When this happens, just trim the body flange after the pot is cast. Lift the lid-and-flange template out, using the holes in it as handles. You've just created the flange

prototype for the inset lid. Clean it up very gently with a soft brush and water.

Place a tapered block of clay in the center of the clay in the mold, being careful not to disturb the flange prototype (see photo 49). This clay block will serve as a pour hole in the finished mold. Make sure the plaster surfaces are well soaped and apply spray mold release. Assemble the plaster-retaining structure and pour plaster over the top of the body mold and around the clay block, up to 1½ inches (3.8 cm) thick. When the plaster has cured, disassem-

ble the mold (see photo 50). Remove the clay, and clean and dry the mold (see page 19).

Andrew Martin

Bountiful, 2006
9½ x 20 x 12 inches (24.1 x 50.8 x 30.5 cm)
Slip-cast porcelain; electric fired, cone 7
Photo by Nick Elias

overhang lid

The flange on this overhang lid hangs down from the lid and fits into the body (see photo 51 and figure 2). Figuring out how to design one was my second breakthrough in developing various methods for making lids. In the example that follows, the proportions are worked out with paper cutouts.

Begin by drawing the body-rim shape on a piece of ⅛-inch-thick (.3 cm) hardboard and cutting it out. Then draw and cut out a lid shape on ¼-inch-thick (.6 cm) hardboard, providing an overhang by making this cutout ½ to 1 inch (1.3 to 2.5 cm) larger at its edge than the body-rim shape. You can make it even larger, if necessary, as fluid glazes

51

Note the flange hanging down from the underside of the lid

will tend to run down the lid and around its underside during glaze firing, sealing the lid to the body. As with inset lids, I use thicker hardboard for the lid template, in order to ensure a strong lid edge. With this type of lid, you can even double the thickness, depending on the aesthetics of the form. In this example, I modeled the lid edge thicker to give it more visual weight.

Cut duplicate templates, from ⅛-inch-thick (.3 cm) hardboard, for the interface between the body and foot. Also cut a single template from ¼-inch-thick (.6 cm) hardboard for the footprint of the form. (This type of form can also be made without a foot.) You should now have a total of five templates. Determine the height of the body and foot, and assemble the templates with wood and nails (see page 41).

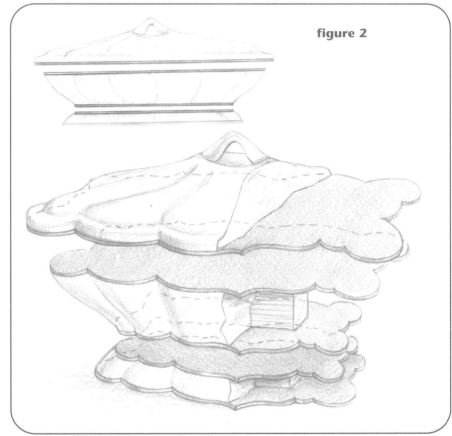

figure 2

Casey O'Connor

Cast Cups, 2005
6 feet x 10 feet x 7 inches (1.8 m x 3 m x 17.8 cm)
Slip-cast earthenware; glaze, decals, china paint
Photo by artist

Dawn Oakford

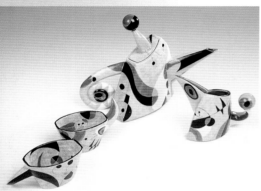

Tea with Miro, 2000
Teapot: 10 x 9 x 11 inches (25.4 x 22.9 x 27.9 cm);
cup: 3 x 5 x 3 inches (7.6 x 12.7 x 7.6 cm);
jug: 5 x 6 x 9 inches (12.7 x 15.2 x 22.9 cm)
Slip cast, stoneware slip; underglaze colors,
cone 7-8
Photo by Uffe Schulze

Evaluating the proportions of the form

Model the body, lid, and foot. Next, model the handle from plastilene and fit it to the form, assembling the parts to see how well their proportions work, and adjusting them if necessary (see photo 52). Then make the molds for the body, lid, foot, and handles. When they are set, empty the molds (see photo 53). Clean the molds and dry them.

For this type of form, the flange is on the lid, and the flange prototype is derived from the interior of the body. As I tried to figure out how to make this type of lid, I realized that casting a mold of the interior of the body would yield a form that would always fit inside the body. If I then attached that plaster casting to the lid, the flange on the lid would always fit inside the body—a simple observation! In practice, you need to cast a mold only for the top ½ inch (1.3 cm) or less of the body in order to align the body with the lid.

To create a prototype for a flange that will fit exactly, you'll take a mold from the inside of a casting of the body. To start making this flange prototype, first refer to the slip-casting instructions on

Removing the prototype from the body mold

pages 132–135. Then prepare the fully dried body mold for casting. Pour slip into the mold (see photo 54). While the slip is absorbing, measure out enough plaster and water to fill the inside of the mold. Allow the casting to get somewhat thicker than normal; this additional thickness will create the play between the lid and body. (Small forms need not be as thick as larger ones.)

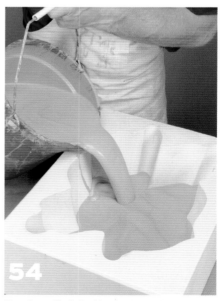

Pouring slip into the body mold

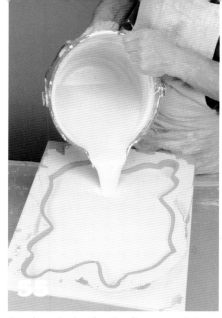

Pouring plaster for the flange prototype

Removing the flange prototype from the casting

Removing the blocking clay and casting from the flange prototype

Next, drain the mold. As soon as the uppermost portion of the casting is no longer liquid, sponge up the excess slip from the casting. The top inner edge of the casting will be sharp. Soften this area with a sponge, rounding it slightly, and smooth away any lumpiness in the casting. Your goal is to eliminate any slight undercuts.

Add the measured plaster to the water and let it soak. If your form is large, save plaster by filling the bottom portion of the casting with blocking clay. This clay will stick to the casting; if you want to prevent this, just cover the bottom of the casting with a layer of plastic. As soon as you can, mix the plaster and fill the casting to the top, being careful not to pour too much plaster (see photo 55). Bounce the table to level the liquid plaster.

Once the plaster is cured, place the body mold on its side. To remove the plaster flange prototype, strike the mold firmly with a rubber mallet. The plaster flange prototype and the casting will begin to slide out (see photo 56). The upper portion of the plaster piece will serve as the flange prototype (see photo 57). Clean it up, removing

any undercuts or irregularities. Make sure that it tapers from the rim to a point 1½ inches (3.8 cm) below the rim. If necessary, use sandpaper or shaving tools to create this taper.

Cut keys in the edge of the lid mold. Soap the flange prototype chunk and the lid mold, and then fill the lid mold with very soft blocking clay. You don't need to fill the middle of the mold with clay, but do make sure that the clay around the rim is level with the edge of the mold, and smooth out the edge with rubber ribs. Place the flange prototype on top of the clay. You should find it easy to visualize the lid with a flange at this point. Make sure the flange prototype is spaced evenly from the edge of the lid mold, and then press it firmly into the soft clay. Use a rubber mallet to drive it in, if necessary (see photo 58). You don't have to press it down very far—just far enough to ensure that the poured plaster won't run underneath it. If there are any gaps between the flange prototype and the clay, add a coil of clay and smooth it off again (see photo 59). Make sure the transition from the soft clay to flange prototype is clean, with no undercuts.

Pounding the flange prototype into the soft clay

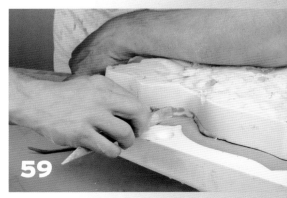

Adding coils to ensure that no plaster runs under the flange prototype

79

Wendy Walgate

Please the Pigs, 2006
11 x 13 x 8 inches (27.9 x 33 x 20.3 cm)
Slip-cast white earthenware; cone 06; postfired
assembly
Photo by artist

Pouring the flange mold

Coat all the plaster with spray mold
release. Set up the plaster-retaining
structure and pour enough plaster to
make this second section of the lid
mold 1½ inches (3.8 cm) thick (see
photo 60). The flange prototype chunk
will stick up out of the poured plaster.
Let the plaster cure, then gently disassemble the two-piece lid mold.

Sometimes the flange prototype just
slides off, but sometimes it sticks to the
clay and requires a little help to separate (see photo 61).

Because the flange mold is ring
shaped, disassembly is a delicate matter. Look at the flange prototype to see
if any plaster has run under its edge
(see photo 62). If this has happened,
carefully cut the plaster away with a
craft knife or scrape it with a metal rib.
Tap the underside of the flange mold
very lightly (don't hit it hard!) with a

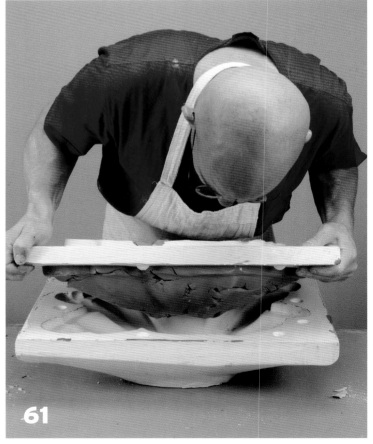

Separating the flange mold from the body mold

small rubber mallet (see photo 63). The flange prototype should begin to loosen and slide out of the mold. If the mold doesn't drop off right away, tap around the edge of its underside.

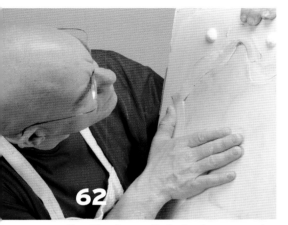

62

Checking to see if plaster has run under the flange prototype

63

Tapping the flange mold to remove the prototype

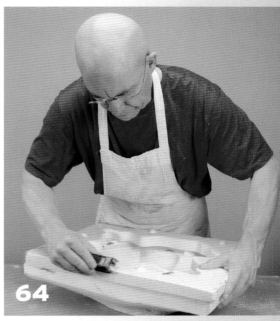

64

Shaving the mold to finish the edges

Andrew Martin

Moveable Feast, 2006
10 ½ x 19 x 14 inches (26.7 x 48.3 x 35.6 cm)
Slip-cast porcelain; electric fired, cone 7
Photo by Nick Elias

Once the flange prototype comes loose, clean up its rough edge. Use vinegar to remove the mold soap, sand the mold, and prepare the finished mold for drying (see photo 64).

cap lid

The flange on this form rises from the body to fit snugly into the lid (see photo 65). One way to make a cap lid involves using templates both for the shape of the pot (top view) and for the profile (side view). This same type of flange is shown in the Cap Lid for the Shoulder of a Teapot (see pages 97–100). Unlike the other forms that I've presented in this book, however, the lobed body prototype is created with templates positioned in vertical, as well as horizontal, alignment.

You'll start by drawing a vertical profile of the form you wish to make. (You don't need to think about the lid or the foot of the jar at this stage—just the profile of the body.) Then you'll decide how many lobed sections you'd like to divide the body into. The jar in this example is composed of six sections. Next, you'll cut templates that will enable you to create an armature for the body (see figure 3). Following is a way to visualize those templates and the way they fit together:

Imagine an apple. If you were to cut this apple in half vertically, its cross-section would represent the full-profile template that you'll cut for the prototype of the body. Now cut the halves of the imaginary apple into six equal-sized sections by making four slices. Each of these four slices represents one

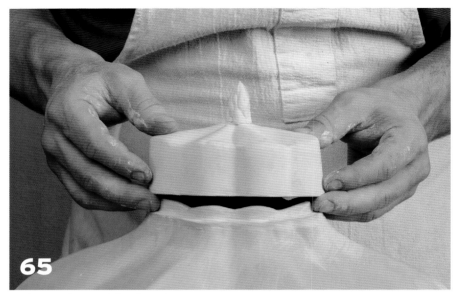

65

Notice the flange rising from the body.

figure 3

82

of the four half-profile templates you'll cut for the body prototype. When you assemble all the templates, the four half-profile templates will radiate outward from the center of the vertical, full-profile template.

First, draw the full-profile template on paper, cut it out, trace it onto hardboard, and cut out the hardboard template. Then make a paper cutout for the half-profile templates and trace it onto hardboard. Use temporary spray adhesive to bond four layers of hardboard together, with the traced half-profile piece on top, and then cut through them simultaneously. Separate the layers to get your four half-profile templates.

The shapes of the templates for the foot and lid are determined by the way in which the body templates are aligned at the top and bottom. Begin by standing the body templates on a sheet of paper, in the desired positions. Hold them in place with wood blocks or a bit of hot glue. Make a mark on the paper at the outer, bottom corner of each template. Repeat this step on another piece of paper, marking the outer top corners of the aligned templates.

Now draw the shape (top view) of the lid, using the marks you just made. Repeat to draw the shape of the foot. Cut out both shapes. Using these paper cutouts, cut two identical foot templates and two identical lid templates from doubled layers of 1/8-inch-thick (.3 cm) hardboard bonded with spray adhesive. Mark the alignment on the pairs of templates before disassembling them so that you'll be able to maintain that alignment when you reassemble the pairs later. In this example, I also cut another template for the footprint of the jar.

You should now have one full template and four half-templates for the profile of the body; these will all be used vertically. You should also have two templates for the lid, two for the foot, and one for the footprint; these will be used horizontally.

To begin assembly of the armature for the body, position the full-profile template on top of the template that will form the floor of the jar. Use a carpenter's square to make sure that the two templates are perpendicular, then glue them together with a hot-glue gun. Align the half-profile templates so that they radiate from the centerline of the full-profile template, then hot-glue them into place, too. Finally, glue one of the two lid templates on top of the assembled armature. Check to make sure the templates are firmly in place (see photo 66).

Construct the armature for the foot with the remaining foot template and the footprint template, in the same way that you made the armature for the plate (see page 41). I know from

66

Gluing the templates in place

Mr. Simon Ward

Seeda, 2001
53 x 38 inches (134.6 x 96.5 cm)
Plaster molded, slip cast; terra cotta and earthenware
Photo by artist

Amy M. Santoferraro

Deer Parade, 2006
24 x 15 x 13 inches (61 x 38.1 x 33 cm)
Slip-cast porcelain; electric fired, cone 6;
mixed media
Photo by artist

experience that the weight of this jar will crush a single-walled foot in the firing, so the two-piece foot mold that I make for this jar creates a hollow-cast form with an exterior foot and an interior foot that bears the jar's weight (see pages 88–89).

Pack clay into the sections of the body armature, working a little into each section at a time. (If you fill one section completely, it will press the templates out of alignment.) When you've finished, you can model the form. To model the lobes that I envisioned for the body, I made a custom rib. Use a similar rib to rake the clay away until the edge of the rib hits the edges of the templates and reveals the contours of the form (see photo 68).

When you've finished modeling the body, model the foot and the lid. Assemble the three parts so that you can evaluate the form as a whole, and make adjustments as necessary. Then wrap up the body prototype in plastic.

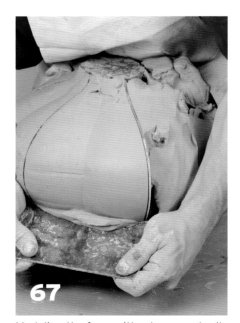

67

Modeling the form with a homemade rib

68

Cutting the plywood that will divide the mold into two sections

Next, make the mold of the lid. (To make the mold for the foot for this jar, refer to the instructions for making hollow-cast feet on pages 88–89.) After cleaning it up and drying it, cast the lid mold slightly thicker than normal and drain it. (For more information, see the chapters on Slip Formulation and Casting.) Remove any roughness on the inside of the casting that might create undercuts and fill the casting with plaster to create the flange prototype. Use wet/dry sandpaper to remove any undercuts in this plaster prototype, then soap it and glue it to the top of the body model with epoxy.

Make sure you keep the alignment of parts straight as you proceed. This flange is cast in the same mold section as the shoulder of the form, and the mold is split horizontally at the widest part of the jar. Because the prototype is so heavy, the first mold section you make will be of the top of the jar instead of the bottom. In order to do this, you'll need to make a platform around the form, into which you'll pour and frost the plaster around the upper portion of the body prototype.

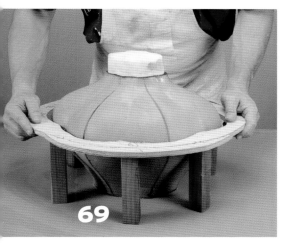

69

Placing the constructed platform around the prototype

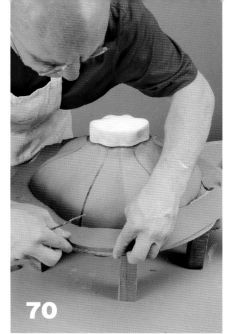

70

Fitting slabs of clay on the plywood ring, around the prototype

71

Filling gaps between the flange and body prototypes

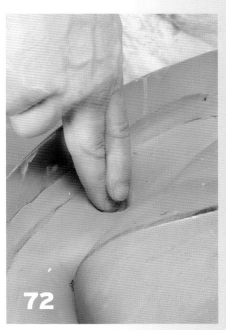

72

Pressing keys into the soft clay

Because I used a custom rib to create the shape (top view) of the jar, I now use it and a marker to create an approximation of the shape on cardboard. Cut this shape out of the cardboard and check to make sure that the hole in the cardboard fits around the widest part of the jar. Adjust the hole until the cardboard fits a bit loosely around the body prototype. Then create a 1½-inch-diameter (3.8 cm) cardboard ring by cutting around the hole you just made. Transfer this ring shape to plywood and cut it out (see photo 68). To build a plywood platform with this ring, cut wooden legs for it that will raise the top of the platform to sit ½ inch (1.3 cm) below the widest dimension of the jar (see photo 69).

When the platform is in place, fit slabs of clay tightly around the upper portion of the form, on the plywood ring (see photo 70). Make sure there are no gaps between the armature and the flange prototype (see photo 71). Also check to see that there's a very clean line where the slab touches the prototype. I took this opportunity to create keys in the slab of plastic clay (see photo 72). I could have carved them into the plaster later, but it's easier to use a thumb or finger to make indentations in the plastic clay at this point.

Judith Salomon

Vases on Black Base, 2005
7 x 8 x 12 inches (17.8 x 20.3 x 30.5 cm)
Slip cast and hand built; cone 04
Photo by Anthony Gray

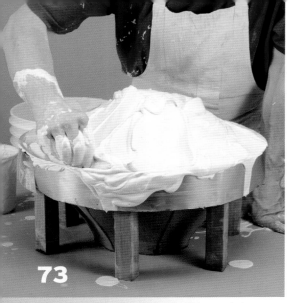

73

Frosting the upper portion of the prototype

74

Pressing the drain tubing into the prototype

Staple flashing to the plywood and seal the vertical seam and the bottom of the flashing with duct tape; the tape will provide added insurance, which you'll need because you'll be pouring plaster into a retaining structure that's suspended in the air. Also press a coil of clay around the edge of the clay slabs where they meet the flashing.

Although I didn't do it in this example, you can also add a piece of clay on top of the flange prototype to act as a reservoir for feeding the form with slip. If you choose to do this, use a mass of clay that tapers from wide at the bottom to narrow on top. Since the top of this mold will lift off the bottom, you don't want an undercut in the reservoir. Make sure that you have an opening wide enough into which to pour the slip.

Apply spray mold release to the flange prototype and to the clay; this will help them release from the body mold when it's finished. To complete this first mold section, pour plaster into the flashing and then frost the rest of the form (see photo 73). Level the top of the mold with a board or shave it to level before it enters the heat cycle.

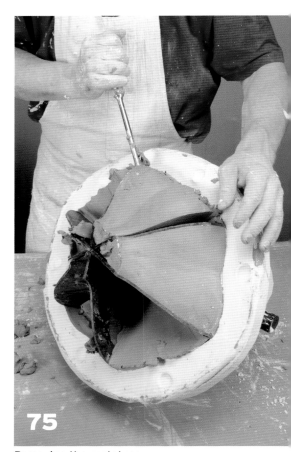

75

Removing the prototype

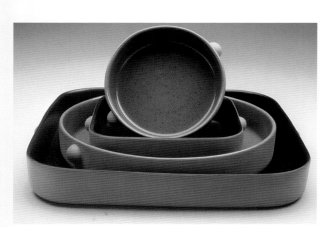

Paul Eshelman

Bump Bowls, 2003
2 ½ x 14 x 13 inches (6.4 x 35.6 x 33 cm)
Slip cast; glazed and unglazed surfaces;
electric fired, cone 4
Photo by artist

Once the plaster is set, remove the flashing, flip the body mold and prototype over, and remove the platform and the blocking clay. Clean up the prototype and soap the plaster. Clean up any damage done to the prototype in the first molding process.

At this point, it's wise to anticipate that the finished mold, filled with slip, will be so heavy that you won't want to lift it to pour out the slip. To avoid having to lift this weight, you'll create a drain at the very bottom of the second mold section; I use drip-feed irrigation tubing with a screw cap. Press the tubing into the prototype (see photo 74). In production, after the slip casting is complete, you'll drain the slip by removing the cap.

Staple flashing to the side of the previous mold section and seal the seam where the two meet by adding a coil of clay. Again, apply spray mold release to the prototype. Then frost the bottom of the jar, just as you did the top. While the plaster is still wet, level the bottom with a board and a bubble level. Disassemble the mold by prying it apart, using a pastry scraper and mallet if necessary, and remove the prototype (see photo 75). The spray that you applied to the prototype should help release it from the mold easily. (Apparently, I did not apply enough!)

Denise Pelletier

Veil, 2003
28 x 16 x 4 inches (71.1 x 40.6 x 10.2 cm)
Slip-cast and altered invalid feeders; black porcelain, etched glass, oxidation, cone 6
Photo by Dean Powell

Andrew Martin

Ode to a Persian Mood, 2006
14 x 13 x 11 inches (35.6 x 33 x 27 cm)
Slip-cast porcelain; electric fired, cone 7
Photo by Nick Elias

hollow-cast feet

For many of my vases, casseroles, and terrine dishes, I make feet that flare out from the body as they come down to meet the table. The simple, one-piece version of this foot is described on pages 44–47 and is sufficient for small forms, but a very heavy form may collapse a foot of this type. The same foot, however, can be reinforced to support a heavy form. The advantage of the foot described in this section is that it is actually two feet. The first one is visible on the exterior of the pot, and the second is a hidden, interior foot that actually bears the weight of the form.

In this example, we'll use the foot prototype from the jar described on pages 82–87. To cast the first mold section, which will create the outer foot, start by positioning the foot prototype upright. Hammer two nails into the hardboard template, at opposite, inner ends (or corners) of the prototype. Cut two pieces of plastic tubing and wrap a thin piece of duct tape around the outside of each one. (The tape will create an undercut that will lock the tubes into the mold when the plaster has set.) Fill the tubes with clay and place one over each nail (see photo 76). Pour plaster to cast the mold section (see photo 77). Remove the prototype when the plaster is set, then cut keys into the rim of the mold.

To create the inner foot prototype, first dust the mold with Chinese dust. This will prevent the plastic clay from sticking to the wet mold. Then fill the mold with clay, leveling it to the top. Place a board on top of the mold, flip the board and mold over, and turn the clay out of the mold, onto the board. Using a needle tool, draw a line on the top surface of the pressed clay, 1¾ inches (4.4 cm) in from its edge.

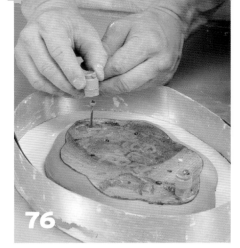

76

Placing the clay-filled tubes over the nails

77

Pouring the first mold section for a hollow-cast foot

Using a needle tool or a fettling knife, cut along this line, flaring the cut toward the outer edge of the form, to a pitch of 5 to 15 degrees (see photo 78). Place the mold back over the clay and flip it over again. Remove the board and then remove the inner clay core that you cut; you'll be left with a ring of clay, still in the mold. You now have the prototype for the hollow-cast foot.

The next mold section that you pour will make the interior of the foot and also the footprint. Before pouring the plaster, ensure that there are no undercuts and that the fill tubes are covered with clay. Clean up with a sponge, soap the mold, apply spray mold release to it, and pour the plaster (see photos 79 and 80). After the plaster has set, empty the mold (see photo 81).

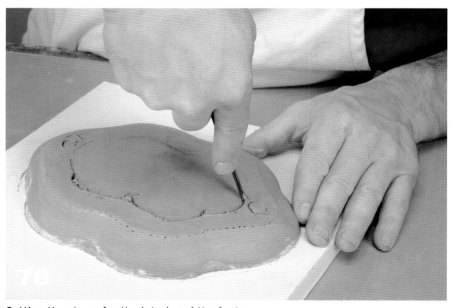

78

Cutting the shape for the interior of the foot

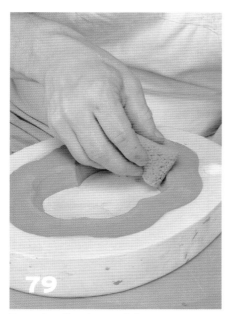

Sponging the clay prototype

Pouring the second section of the hollow-cast foot

Removing the foot prototype from the mold

Jesse Ross

Cup and Saucer, 2006
6 x 5 x 5 inches (15.2 x 12.7 x 12.7 cm)
Porcelain; reduction bisque, cone 7; electric glaze, cone 04
Photo by artist

82

83

84

Making a clean line around the artichoke

Removing the blocking clay

Pinning cone-shaped pour spouts to the stems of the artichokes

fruits & vegetables

Making molds of fruits and vegetables is always an aesthetic choice; you'll want to consider the inherent qualities of the object and how they relate to the work. Over the years I've used bell peppers, asparagus, strawberries, jalapeño peppers, okra, and artichokes. Some of my ideas have worked both aesthetically and in practice; others haven't work in actual practice.

Most fruits and vegetables are somewhat symmetrical and lend themselves to casting with two-piece molds. To start the mold for an artichoke, first fill the spaces under the leaves with soft clay and then clean off the excess. Then bury the artichoke halfway in clay, with the dividing line at the widest section. Ensure that the line where the clay and the artichoke meet is very clean (see photo 82). Press keys into the soft clay, assemble the cottles around the piece, and pour the plaster. No soap or spray mold release is needed at this stage.

When the plaster has set, remove the cottles and the blocking clay (see photo 83). Clean up the plaster, soap it, and apply spray mold release. Cut

small clay cones and pin them to the bottoms of the stems to act as pour spouts when the mold is cast (see photo 84). When these are in place, replace the cottles and pour the second mold section.

After the mold has gone through the heat cycle, disassemble it and remove the artichoke and the clay funnels (see photo 85). To clean the interior of the mold, just use a soft brush to remove any residual clay from the casting surface. Remove the mold soap with vinegar, finish the exterior as you would any other mold, and set the mold aside to dry.

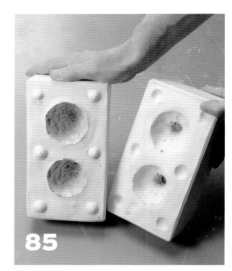
85

The finished artichoke mold

Andrew Martin

Quadchroma 'Chokes, 2006
4 x 4 x 4 inches (10.2 x 10.2 x 10.2 cm)
Slip-cast porcelain; electric fired, cone 7
Photo by Nick Elias

no-model molds

One of my first molds was made without a fully modeled prototype. Tom Spleth had told me that he just carved the plaster to make a mold directly. Following is a description of how to make a basic plaster mold and carve an image into it.

To use this technique, start by pouring a slab of plaster to serve as a base. When the plaster has set, carve keys in each corner and clean up the plaster. Next, apply mold soap to the base and place a block of clay in its center, leaving about 3 inches (7.6 cm) between each edge of the base and the block of clay. This will give you a mold thick enough to carve. Apply spray mold release to the plaster base (see photo 86).

Mix and pour plaster around the block of clay. After the plaster has set, disassemble the cottles (see photo 87). Then remove the base of the mold, using a pastry scraper and hammer if necessary (see photo 88). Remove the block of clay (see photo 89). Reassemble the mold for drying.

86

Spraying mold release on the plaster

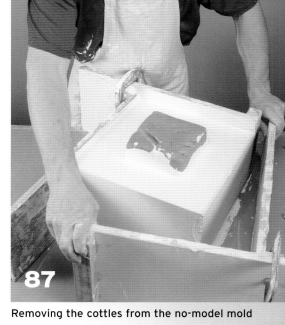

87

Removing the cottles from the no-model mold

88

Separating the base of the mold with a scraper

89

Removing the block of clay

Denise Pelletier

Mute, 2004
2 x 9 x 12 feet (0.6 x 2.7 x 3.7 m)
Slip-cast and altered invalid feeders;
black porcelain, oxidation, cone 6
Photo by John Carlano

When the mold is completely dry, remove the base and file out the plaster with a wood rasp to create the form of the pot (see photo 90). Be careful not to make any undercuts. To finish the mold, sand the casting surface with wet/dry sandpaper (see photo 91). The casting you make with this mold should slip right out, but if you have problems removing it, alter the mold further and resand it.

Richard Shaw

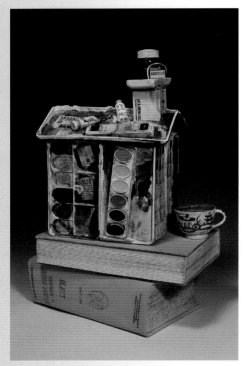

House with Canton Cup, 2004
17 x 11 ³⁄₄ x 8 inches (42.3 x 29.8 x 20.3 cm)
Slip-cast porcelain; glaze, cone 6; glaze, overglaze, cone 018, decals
Photo by Lesley Baker

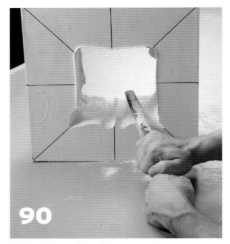

90

Filing the mold with a wood rasp

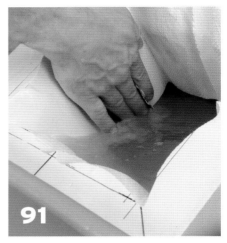

91

Wet sanding the rough mold

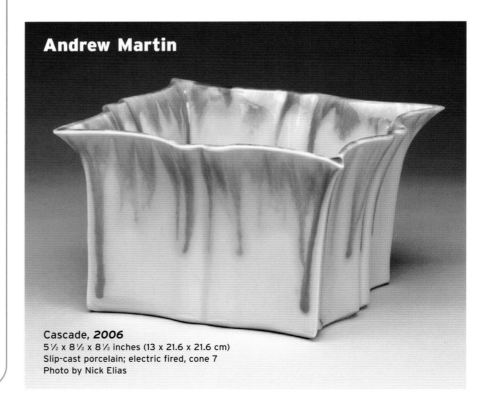

Andrew Martin

Cascade, *2006*
5 ¹⁄₂ x 8 ¹⁄₂ x 8 ¹⁄₂ inches (13 x 21.6 x 21.6 cm)
Slip-cast porcelain; electric fired, cone 7
Photo by Nick Elias

MAKING COMPLEX MOLDS

Visualizing how to make a complex mold is like mapping a three-dimensional puzzle. The pieces of these molds fit together perfectly and, like puzzle pieces, will fit only one way. No matter how you construct a complex mold, you should always make sure that you can disassemble it in the reverse order from which you made it. Undercut parts of the mold that indent the casting will be the last made and the first removed.

rim-to-rim cap lid

The flange on this form rises from the body and fits perfectly into the lid (see photo 92). To make a lid and body that meet rim to rim (see figure 4), first draw the shape of the rim on paper, then transfer the shape onto two hard-

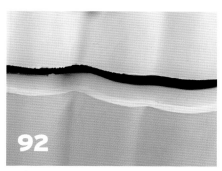

92

Notice the flange rising from the body

board templates. Next, rough cut the templates and bind them together with spray adhesive. Then use a jigsaw to cut them to their finished shape. Before separating the templates, mark one side "lid clay here" and the other "body clay here," then pull them apart. Model the lid and body on these templates; pack the clay first and then use a cheese cutter to remove the excess (see photo 93). Place the two proto-

types together while modeling them in order to check their proportions in relation to each other (see photo 94). When you've achieved the desired prototype proportions, you'll make the molds for each piece.

To make the body mold, first pour a flat plaster base that is 1½ inches (3.8 cm) larger than the template at its

93

Removing excess clay with a cheese cutter

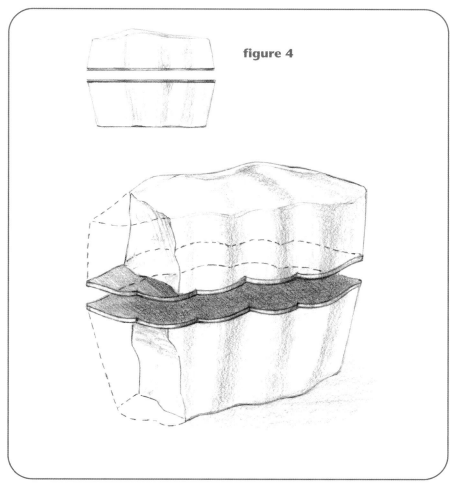

figure 4

94

Preparing to check the proportions of the lid and body

95

The lid and body prototypes ready for casting

96

Scraping the plaster level to the top of the template

97

Sanding the two molds together to remove the template marks

edge. Cut keys in this piece, soap it, and place the body prototype on it, standing right side up (see photo 95). Assemble cottles around the prototype and pour plaster up to the top edge of the template; this will form the second section of the body mold. When the plaster begins to firm up (see page 31), scrape off any excess by running a straightedge rib across the template to make a flush, horizontal edge where the edge of the mold section and the template meet (see photo 96).

Unless there are undercuts in the lid prototype, you can make the lid mold by simply covering the prototype with plaster. When the plaster is fully set, turn the lid mold over and check to see if any plaster has run underneath the template. If it has, scrape it off with a rib. Then remove the templates from both the body and lid molds, being very careful not to chip the plaster. Remove the lid and body prototypes.

The templates will have left marks in the molds. To get rid of these, place the lid and second body-mold sections together, upside down, leaving the base of the body mold unattached. Align the two molds as closely as possible in the sink or a tub of water, then run water into the mold. Reach

through the bottom and sand the two parts simultaneously to remove the template marks (see photo 97). Doing this will ensure that the lid and body match up as closely as possible, which will eliminate having to clean up the template marks on each pot.

Blowing to check the thickness of the casting

To make the prototype for the flange, start by drying the lid mold and then filling it with casting slip. As with all the lids, cast the lid slightly thicker than normal. Blow on the liquid slip to check the thickness of the casting (see photo 98). After draining the mold (see photo 99), wait until the slip has lost its sheen, then smooth away the sharp interior edge and any other roughness. Fill the casting with plaster (see photo 100). Once the plaster flange prototype is set, remove it from the lid mold (see photo 101). Clean it up and sand it to remove any undercuts.

Assemble the body mold and its base. Cut keys in the top edge of the body mold and fill it with clay, making the clay smooth, flat, and flush with the

99

Draining the mold

100

Filling the casting with plaster

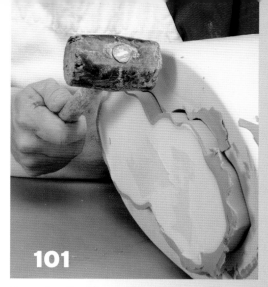

101

Removing the flange prototype from the lid mold

rim (see photo 102). Soap the top of the mold and the flange prototype (see photo 103). Place the flange prototype on the soft clay in the body mold. Exact registration is very important on this type of lid. If the lid and body are out of registration, the lid will sit to one side, leaving the flange exposed on the other side. Though the casting can be manipulated slightly, try to avoid this by making sure there is equal space between the flange prototype and the body mold. (When I've made the mistake of failing to check this space, I've simply made a new flange mold. Just make sure to keep the flange prototype.)

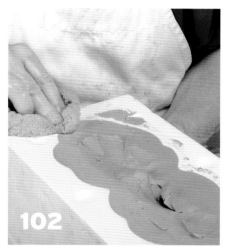

102

Cleaning off the residual clay from the scraping process

103

Soaping the flange prototype

Ilena Finocchi

***Straight Line Is Also a Circle (Part C)*, 2005**
4 x 24 x 24 inches (10.2 x 61 x 61 cm)
Modeled feathers; black porcelain; cone 6
Photo by artist

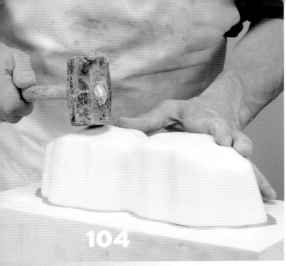

104

Pounding the flange prototype into the soft clay

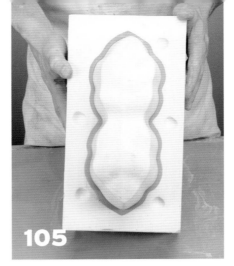

105

The correct alignment of the flange prototype

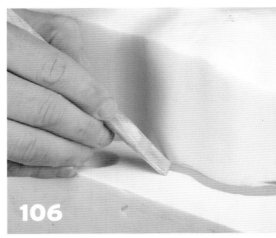

106

Filling gaps between the flange prototype and the soft clay

When the flange prototype is exactly in place, tap it firmly into the clay with a rubber mallet so that plaster will not run underneath it (see photo 104). Be sure the flange prototype is still aligned correctly with the body (see photo 105).

If pressing the prototype into the clay has deformed it, smooth the clay and fill any gaps where the clay and the plaster meet (see photo 106). Apply spray mold release to the top of the mold and the flange prototype. Pour the flange section to 1½ inches (3.8 cm) in thickness (see photo 107). Check the depth of the plaster with one finger. To remove the flange prototype from the flange mold, tap the bottom of the flange mold very gently with a rubber mallet. Unless there are undercuts, the prototype should slide out easily. The other mold sections have already been cleaned, so just remove the soap from the flange mold with vinegar, finish it with wet/dry sandpaper, and reassemble the mold for drying (see photo 108).

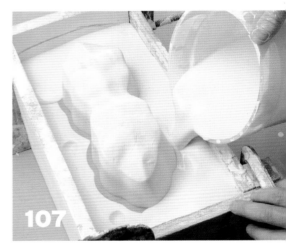

107

Pouring the flange mold

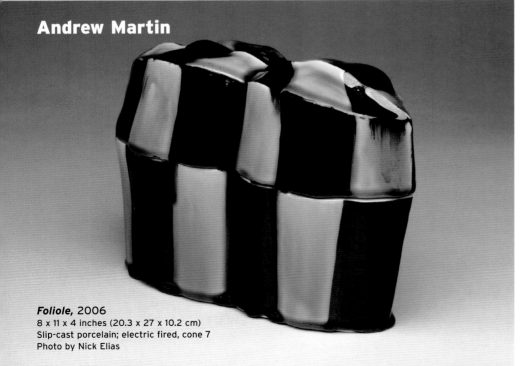

Andrew Martin

Foliole, 2006
8 x 11 x 4 inches (20.3 x 27 x 10.2 cm)
Slip-cast porcelain; electric fired, cone 7
Photo by Nick Elias

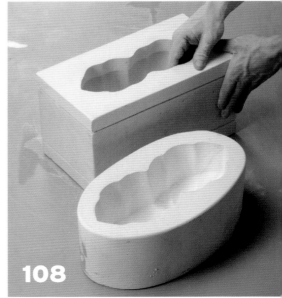

108

The finished and assembled mold

cap lid for
the shoulder of a teapot

The flange on this form extends upwards from the body to fit into the lid (see photo 109). This type of lid sits on the shoulder of a form, such as a teapot or a Chinese ginger jar (see figure 5). Much like the jar mold we made previously, this mold is split into two halves because there are undercuts in the sides of the form. Six templates are cut: two identical ones for the floor and foot interface, one for the foot-print, one for the shoulder, and two

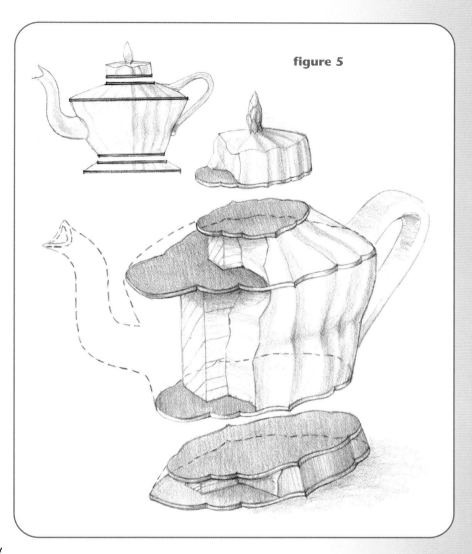

figure 5

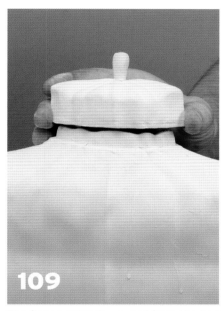

109

The flange extends upward from the body

Paul Eshelman

Individual Teapots, 2005
5 x 9 x 4 inches (12.7 x 22.9 x 10.2 cm)
Slip cast; glazed and unglazed surfaces;
electric fired, cone 4
Photo by artist

97

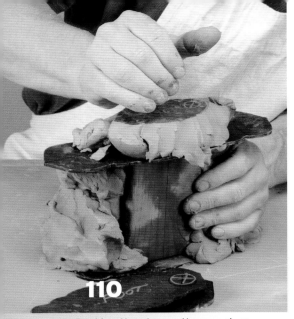

110

Packing the clay on the armature

111

Modeling the form with a homemade rib

112

Checking the proportions of all the prototypes

more identical ones for the lid and the lid seat. The body form is assembled from three of these templates: the floor, the shoulder, and the lid seat. The foot armature is assembled from the foot interface and the footprint template. The remaining template is for the lid. Remember to mark your templates (see pages 41 and 45) so that you can align them correctly later.

Begin modeling the prototypes by packing the armatures with clay (see photo 110). Then model the clay with a cheese cutter and custom-made wooden ribs (see photo 111). After

modeling all the prototypes, test their relationships to one another (see photo 112). Wrap up the body prototype in plastic and make the molds for the lid and the foot. After cleanup and drying, cast the lid mold slightly thicker than normal and drain it. Fill the casting with plaster to create the flange prototype. Sand the plaster to eliminate any undercuts, soap the flange prototype, and use epoxy to glue it to the top of the body prototype. Make sure you keep the alignment of parts straight as you proceed. Because this mold will split vertically, the flange is cast in the same mold section as the body of the form.

For the teapot body, begin by making a separate plaster base, with keys cut into two long edges. Soap it, apply spray mold release, and place the body prototype on the base. On this form, I put a tapered piece of clay on top of the flange prototype to create a reservoir. Block off half the form with clay (see photo 113). Assemble cottles around the form and pour plaster to

Heather Mae Erickson

Sprinkle, 2006
2 x 6 x 8 inches (5 x 15.2 x 20.3 cm)
Plaster models, porcelain slip; cone 6, reduction
Photo by Ken Yanoviak

113 Blocking off half the form with clay

114 Pouring the first side of the body mold

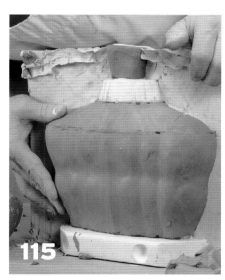

115 Removing the blocking clay

116 Pouring the second side of the body mold

near the top of the flange prototype (see photo 114).

When the plaster has set, separate the two sections and remove the blocking clay (see photo 115). Clean up and soap the mold. Because the prototype must sit flush to the base, the first plaster mold section was cast vertically.

Now that the plaster base and first mold section are locked together, the third mold section can be cast with the prototype in a horizontal position (see photo 116). When the plaster has set, remove the cottles from the mold.

Separate the mold's two side sections and remove the prototype (see photos

Ron Nagle

Cracker Boy, 2005
3 x 5 ⅛ x 3 ¾ inches (7.6 x 13 x 9.5 cm)
Slip-cast earthenware; overglaze, decal
Photo by Don Tuttle

117 and 118). Then reassemble the mold without the base. Just as you would when cleaning up a rim-to-rim cap lid, reach inside the mold to sand the seam where the two sections meet. Disassemble the mold and sand away the template mark at the shoulder. Be very careful not to change the shape of the top or bottom rims of the mold, because they align to the foot and lid. Altering them will alter how the foot and lid fit.

The teapot body shown in this section could have a number of different handles and spouts—or a neck to turn it into a vase. On the basic form, you could have two possible spouts, two possible handles, and three possible spout locations. This gives you six different possible teapot designs. The foot, which is optional, doubles the possibilities to twelve. A further variation would be to sculpt a neck on the lid template to make the form into a vase. The addition of a neck and a foot adds two more possibilities to this basic form. The vase could have a handle and spout, turning it into a ewer. Finally, it could simply be cast as a jar, with or without the foot, bringing the total possible combinations up to seventeen.

117
Separating the mold with a scraper

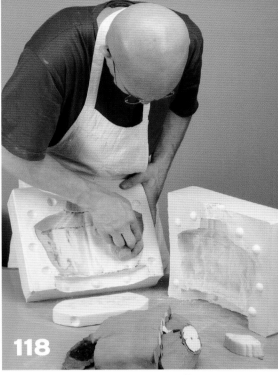
118
Cleaning the mold with a sponge after removing the prototype

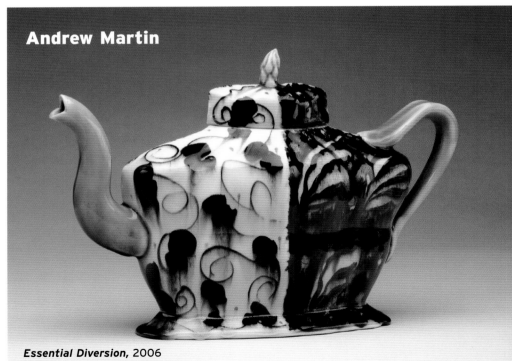
Andrew Martin

Essential Diversion, 2006
9 ½ x 12 x 3 ½ inches (15.2 x 7.6 x 7.6 cm)
Slip-cast porcelain; electric fired, cone 7
Photo by Nick Elias

making a six-piece mold

Teapots are particularly complex forms, but in order to be a teapot, first a teapot must simply be a pot. The teapot body is the stage from which all the secondary forms are animated; it must therefore work aesthetically and functionally as a pot before all the elements that make it a teapot are added. The instructions that follow will show you how to make this teapot—with a lid that fits perfectly (see photo 119).

Refer to previous sections of this book for instructions on how to make spouts, handles, feet, and an inset lid. This lid is made after the body mold is made. Make the prototype for the body from solid clay, or model clay on frames constructed from templates. Make your handle and spout prototypes from plastilene and fit them to the body prototype. Once you've completed the prototypes, you're ready to map out the mold design. My *Rock Teapot* (page 105), for example, requires a six-piece mold for the body. This mold has a base, four mold pieces that form the walls, and one piece that forms the small shoulder and inset flange.

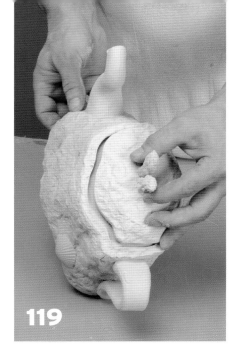

119

The teapot, showing the relationship between the lid and flange

Cast a plaster base and cut keys in it. Next, soap the plaster and place the prototype on the base (see photo 120). To make the first two wall sections, block off the narrow ends of the prototype with clay. Assemble the cottle boards, leaving 1½ inches (3.8 cm) between the base and the cottle boards. The two mold sections you're about to pour will key to the edge of the base when the plaster is cast. Now pour the plaster to create the two mold sections (see photo 121). After the

120

Evaluating the prototypes with the body on its plaster base

121

Pouring the first of two wall sections

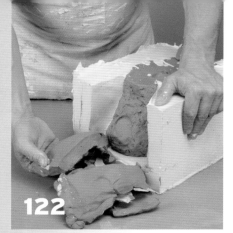

122

Removing the blocking clay

123

Sliding and locking keys hold the next mold section in place.

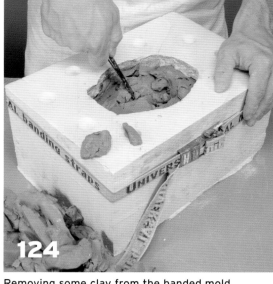

124

Removing some clay from the banded mold

plaster is set, clean off the blocking clay (see photo 122). Sponge off the plaster. Don't remove the prototype until the mold is finished.

To create the final two sections of the wall, start by cutting keys in the ends and top surfaces of the first two side sections; I used sliding keys in this example (see photo 123). Soap the mold and place cottles around the base, again leaving 1½ inches (3.8 cm) between the base and the cottle boards. Next, pour plaster to form the last two wall sections.

As soon as you've taken the cottles off the mold, place a nylon mold strap around it and cinch it tight. Don't disassemble the mold or remove the body prototype yet. Using a loop tool and fettling knife, remove about 1 inch (2.5 cm) of clay from the top of the

mold (see photo 124). Sand the top of the mold and cut two keys in each of the side sections in preparation for making the flange mold for the lid. Soap the mold well.

Place a piece of paper over the opening in the mold and take a tracing of the mold's top edge (see photo 125). Draw a line inside the rim line; it will become the shape of the lid and flange (see photo 126). Cut this shape from ¼-inch-thick (.6 cm) hardboard. Either cut a hole in the center or drive a screw through it to act as a handle.

Fill the mold with soft clay, leaving a recess in the middle. Then smooth and level the clay at the edges, about 1 inch (2.5 cm) in from the edge of the mold. Apply Chinese dust or baby powder to the lid/flange template and to the soft clay (see photo 127). Align

the lid/flange template with the edges of the mold and pound it into place with a rubber mallet; the displaced clay will fill the recess and rise in the area between the template and mold (see photo 128). Cut away this excess clay.

When the top of the template is flush to the top of the mold, lift it out. Once you've removed the template, you'll be able to see the area where the lid will fit. Now place the template back into the clay and check the fit. Shift the template back and forth slightly to create a bit of play in the lid and help it to fit more easily (see photo 129). As the plaster erodes, your lids will get bigger and your flanges smaller, so the lids will get tighter over time.

Linda Cordell

Lambi: Accidental Exposure, 2005
15 x 25 x 10 inches (38.1 x 63.5 x 25.4 cm)
Modeled and hand-built porcelain slip; resin;
cone 10, reduction
Photo by artist

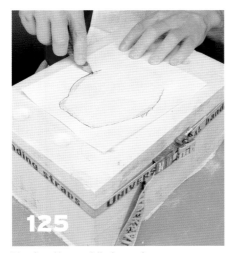

125

Tracing the mold's top edge

126

The inner ring is the shape of the lid and flange

127

Applying baby powder to the soft clay and the template

128

Pounding the template into the soft clay

129

Shifting the template to give the lid some play

Richard Shaw

House of Pencils with Watercolor Box, 2003
8 x 13 ½ x 10 ¼ inches (20.3 x 34.3 x 26 cm)
Slip-cast porcelain; slab built; cone 6, glaze, cone 18
Photo by Anthony Cunha

Jesse Ross

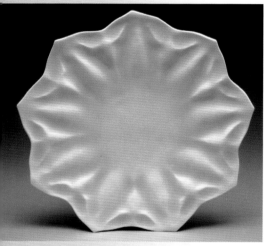

Plate, 2006
9 x 9 x ½ inches (22.9 x 22.9 x 1.27 cm)
Slip-cast porcelain; reduction bisque, cone 7,
electric glaze, cone 04
Photo by artist

130

Placing the funnel in the mound of clay

131

Pouring plaster around the funnel

132

Disassembling the mold to remove the prototype

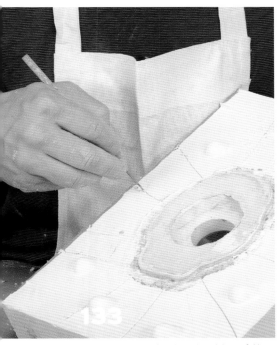

Cutting air vents in the shoulder of the flange mold

Build a small mound of clay in the middle of the flange area and place a large-mouthed funnel in its center (see photo 130). This mound will help the air escape more easily. Use a fine-bristle brush to smooth any roughness in the flange seat. Apply mold soap and spray mold release to the plaster. Pour plaster around the funnel (see photo 131). It can be put in place for casting and then removed easily.

Andrew Martin

Aqua-Terra-Flora, 2006
6 ½ x 11 x 5 ½ inches (16.5 x 27 x 13 cm)
Slip-cast porcelain; electric fired, cone 7
Photo by Nick Elias

When the plaster has set, disassemble the mold (see photo 132). Next remove the mold soap with vinegar, sand the outside of the mold, reassemble it, and set it aside to dry.

After the flange is complete, model the lid form on the template. Make a one-piece mold of this prototype. After the plaster goes through the heat cycle, remove the template and mototype from the lid mold, sand the outside, and dry it as well. To prevent air from being trapped inside the flange mold as you fill it with casting slip, make *vents* by scratching the underside (see photo 133).

Lesley Baker

Grotesque #9, 2004
7 x 7 x 5 inches (17.8 x 17.8 x 12.7 cm)
Slip-cast and assembled porcelain; laser decals, cone 6
Photo by artist

master molds

master molds

Master molds are used to duplicate working molds for production. When I'm considering whether to make a master mold, I have to decide whether doing so will be worth my time. I don't usually duplicate molds with more than two pieces because so much work is involved, but if you plan to use complex molds for production, making a master mold may be well worth the effort. One-piece molds or molds of forms that you need to cast in high quantities are the best to duplicate.

THE ADVANTAGES OF MASTER MOLDS

Years ago I had just started a new semester as a teacher. One evening I arrived back at the studio to a message from the owner of a gallery that represents my work. She told me that a client wanted a 12-piece dinnerware setting—and wanted it delivered in two weeks. Her question was this: "Can you do it?" Because I had all the molds, I took the commission and delivered on time. In fact, I cast 144 dinnerware pieces by the end of the next day—the 72 pieces that the client had ordered—and another full set just in case anything went wrong. I couldn't have completed this job if I hadn't already made dinnerware master molds and cast working molds from them.

Unless I'm going to be making dozens of identical cast pieces, I don't need a lot of working molds; I'd rather spend my time designing new molds for new forms. The only master molds I make are for dinnerware. When I make a set of dishes, my client usually wants a dozen of each piece. If I had only one mold of each piece, it would take me three to four days to cast them all, but with 12 working molds of each dinnerware piece and 18 cup-and-saucer molds, I can cast all the pieces in one day.

I've noticed that over time, artists become better at arriving at simple solutions. As I've already indicated, you should have a compelling reason to make a master mold. In the examples that follow, I demonstrate making a plaster master mold for plates and a rubber master mold for handles. I don't typically make rubber masters for han-

dles because handle tolerances are less exacting than plate tolerances. I find it easier and less time consuming to make a half-dozen working handle molds than a master; the cast handles can vary slightly. With plates, however, a master is necessary because differences from plate to plate will be noticeable.

Rubber is the way to go when you're going to be making many molds of similar forms. Recently I haven't been thinking in terms of producing lines of standard ware, so I've gravitated away from using rubber. Having said that, I'll probably have a pressing need for a rubber master right away!

One of the advantages of a master mold is that irregularities in the original mold can be removed from the master— a real time saver when it comes to cleaning up dinnerware. For example, you can cut bevels on a dinner-plate master, where the wall of the plate meets the floor, eliminating the need to bevel each individual plate. Most potters never wear out their molds, but if you do, you can make master molds from them and cast new working molds from the masters.

I've used different types of master molds over the years but have settled on two types: simple plaster masters and rubber masters. Each material offers different benefits. Plaster master molds are made with Hydrocal gypsum cement, which is very durable and will withstand the abuse of casting working molds. Rubber is an incredible material; among other things, it will accommodate forms with slight undercuts. I duplicate two-piece handle molds with a rubber master.

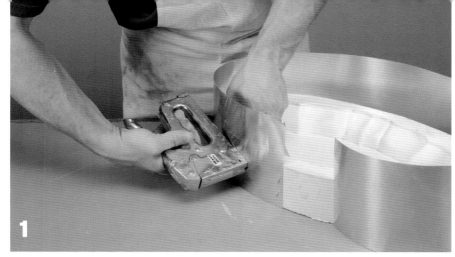

1

Stapling the flashing to the plaster mold

MAKING A PLASTER MASTER MOLD

To duplicate dinnerware molds such as bowls, plates, cups, and saucers, I use simple Hydrocal master molds. These forms are all one-piece molds, as are the masters for them. The plaster master mold described here is one for the plate form on pages 41–43.

2

Pouring Hydrocal into the original mold (soon to be a waste mold)

To produce a simple plaster master, first ensure that the mold is clean. Sand away any rough spots with wet/dry sandpaper in order to make the casting surface as smooth as possible. Also remove any undercuts. Fill any large or small holes in the mold with plastilene. Soap the mold to seal it, then apply spray mold release. If the mold is square or rectangular, assemble cottles around it. If the mold is any other shape, use flashing to assemble the plaster-retaining structure (see photo 1). Use small coils of clay to seal the corners where the upper edges of the mold meet the interior wall of the flashing. Level the mold by placing a small level on top of it, and adjust the mold with shims or balls of clay. Place another, larger coil of clay around the exterior of the plaster-retaining structure, where it meets the work surface.

Make the master by filling the original mold with Hydrocal, 1½ inches (3.8 cm) past the top of the mold (see photo 2). This additional plaster will serve as a base to which flashing can be attached when you make the working molds. The Hydrocal will yield a master mold of incredible density and hardness. Because it expands during the heat stage of its setting cycle, it will often crack the original mold; you may even hear the cracking sound. Don't be concerned; this original mold has become a waste mold.

Ron Nagle

Stratschmear, 2005
3 ¾ x 3 ¾ x 3 ½ inches (9.5 x 9.5 x 8.9 cm)
Slip-cast porcelain; overglaze, decal
Photo by Don Tuttle

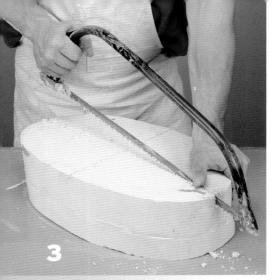

3

Making perpendicular cuts in the waste mold

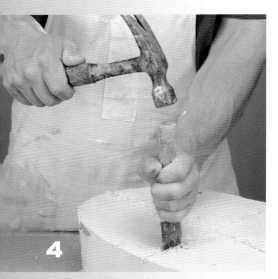

4

Chiseling the plaster along the cuts

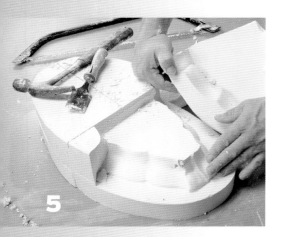

5

Removing the waste mold from the master mold

After the Hydrocal has cured, remove the original mold and inspect the master. Because the master will have expanded, the original mold may be very difficult to remove. If it won't separate easily from the master, use a bow saw to make two perpendicular cuts in it, across the center (see photo 3). Hammer a chisel into the cut, then pry the waste mold apart (see photos 4 and 5). It will break when you do this.

If you used a template to make the rim of the original prototype, eliminate any undercuts in the master by tapering the rim area slightly with a small loop tool. Bevel the area of the master that will shape the bottom edge of the plate in the working mold (see photo 6). Small pores in the original mold will show up as small bumps on the master, so use 600-grit wet/dry sandpaper to remove these, as well as any residual evidence of the template and other flaws. Fill any bubble holes with plastilene, smoothing it to the form. Soap the master, apply spray mold release,

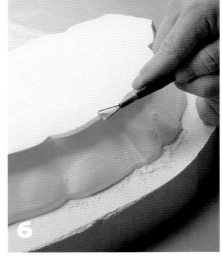

6

Beveling the plaster master mold

assemble the flashing or cottles around it, and pour the first working mold. When it has gone through the heat cycle, remove the working mold from the master (see photo 7).

A slight residue of plaster will stick to the master with each casting of it. Wipe this off with a soft cloth, such as an old T-shirt. Before each subsequent casting, resoap the master and apply spray mold release to it.

7

Removing the working mold from the master mold

MAKING A RUBBER MASTER MOLD

A rubber master mold and a *mother mold* (the plaster mold that supports the master) are used to duplicate a more complicated mold, such as a handle mold.

Rubber is an excellent master material because it picks up details very well. Many different types of rubber are available from industrial sources; check your local ceramic supplier to see which ones they carry, or check online. I've experimented with numerous brands over the years. I like the silicone rubbers, which are very tough and, unlike latex rubbers, will last for many years. I use a two-part rubber compound that is mixed 1:1 by weight and poured onto the mold to be reproduced.

Different rubbers have different qualities. Some can be poured and some can be frosted on like putty. I first started making complex rubber molds by frosting the rubber onto the bowl forms that I wanted to reproduce. The rubber I used at the time, and that I recommend, had to be applied in layers. It would adhere to itself, so there was no need to worry about adhesion of the layers.

Applying spray mold release to the original mold

Pressing a coil of clay between the original mold and the cottle

To make a rubber master mold for a handle, begin by applying several layers of mold soap to the two sections of the handle mold. Assemble cottles around each of the mold sections. Then apply spray mold release to the mold (see photo 8). Seal the seams between the inner walls of the cottles and the upper edges of the mold by pressing narrow

coils of clay into these corners (see photo 9). Because rubber remains liquid for a long time, limiting any leakage is important. A small plaster leak can be quickly sealed, and plaster sets very quickly, as well. Rubber, however, is a very different material; it will often stay liquid for an hour or more. If it starts to leak, it may continue to leak.

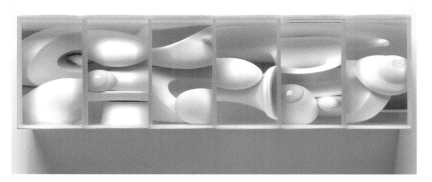

Julie York

Untitled, 2006
15 x 4 ½ x 4 inches (38.1 x 11.4 x 10.2 cm)
Porcelain slip; electric fired, cone 6
Photo by John Carlono

109

Simon Ward

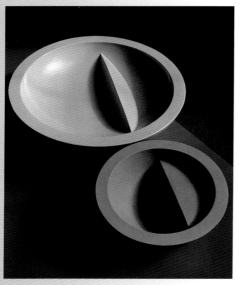

Eclipse Bowls, 2001
24 x 8 inches (61 x 20.3 cm)
Plaster molded, earthenware; electric fired
Photo by artist

10

Pouring the rubber over the original mold

11

Roughing up the rubber as it stiffens

Apply spray mold release to the cottles. Mix the rubber compounds together according to the manufacturer's recommendation, then pour the rubber over the mold (see photo 10). Make sure the rubber covers the uppermost portions of plaster quite thickly; the masters you're making must be thick enough not to tear when you remove them from the working master molds.

Check for leaks around the edge of the cottles. As the rubber begins to stiffen up, you must add some texture to its exposed surface by creating small peaks in it. Do this by poking a stick or a similar implement into the rubber and pulling it out repeatedly (see photo 11). The more texture the better. When you pour the plaster to create a mother mold on top of the rubber, these peaks will act as the keys that lock the rubber master and mother mold together.

When the rubber is very firm, cover it with a layer of plaster 1 inch (2.5 cm) thick (see photo 12). You now have a rubber sandwich of sorts, with plaster bread. The working mold is on the bottom, the rubber master is on top of it, and the mother mold is on the very top. Let the plaster set and then disassemble the cottles. If the rubber has stuck to the cottles, cut it away with a craft knife. Remove the mother mold from the rubber, then remove the rubber from the original mold (see photo 13). Clean the original working mold with vinegar. The original mold won't have been affected by the master-mold-making process; you can use it for production.

To cast a new working mold from the master you've made, first dilute some dish soap with water, mixing one part soap to 10 parts water. Fill a spray bottle with this solution and apply it to

12

Pouring the plaster mother mold

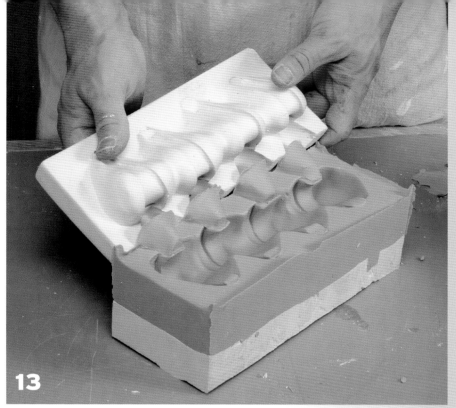

13

Removing the original mold from the rubber master

the portions of the rubber master that will be covered by plaster. The solution will reduce the surface tension of the rubber, so air bubbles will release more easily from its surface.

Let the rubber master mold air dry, place it in the mother mold, assemble the cottles around the molds, and cast the new plaster working mold. When

the plaster has set, remove it from the rubber.

Be sure to dry the two sections of the new working mold together. If there's any distortion in the rubber master and therefore in the new working mold, drying them together may help the pieces warp back together.

Before casting another working mold from the rubber master, use vinegar and water to remove any plaster residue from the rubber. Store the rubber master with the mother mold in a cool, dry place. I keep them dust-free by covering them with a sheet of plastic.

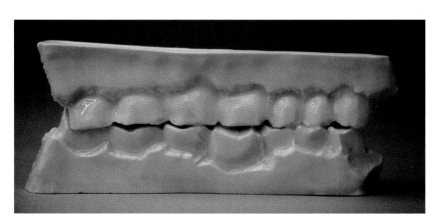

David Alban

Teeth, **2004**
1½ x 6 x 1 inches (3.8 x 15.2 x 2.5 cm)
Cast bone china
Photo by artist

Donna Polseno
& Richard Hensley
slip casting in production

Donna Polseno

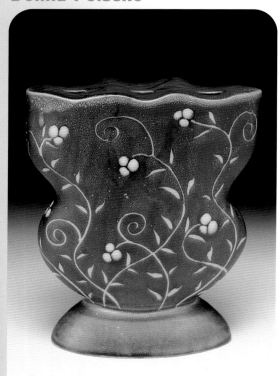

Untitled, 2006
12 x 8 x 5 inches (30.5 x 20.3 x 12.7 cm)
Slip cast; electric fired; multiple glazes using wax resist, cone 4
Photo by Tim Barnwell

Although Donna and Richard (Rick) had been exposed to mold making while they were in school, they didn't start using molds until much later. After spending many years as studio artists, Rick took a teaching position

at Kent State University, and he and Donna got involved with molds during this time. Donna was making pots for a living, as well as laboriously constructed hand-built forms. She and Rick realized that they couldn't make a living from her individually created pieces alone, even if Donna made them smaller, so Rick suggested that Donna make some of her one-of-a-kind pieces smaller—and then make molds of them. Donna agreed because she was looking for another way to make a living besides making sculptures.

At the time Danny Mehlman, a friend from the Rhode Island School of Design, was making a living as a master mold maker. Rick and Donna visited him in New York, and Donna brought a model and asked Danny how to make molds. That's how she and Rick got started.

When Donna and Rick first started slip casting, they weren't aiming for a particular quality that only slip casting could offer. After hand building for so many years, Donna was attracted to the time-saving qualities of mold

making, and to the fact that slip casting allows the artist to make complicated, textured forms.

Not long after she started to slip cast, Donna realized that firing could produce truly beautiful slip-cast pieces. She and Rick developed a slip that fired to cone 7 and that was translucent. "It was just really beautiful," she says. And it was very different from their previous work in raku, stoneware, and porcelain.

When Rick was asked about a lobed teapot that he'd made when he first started casting—an excellent example of what can be done with molds—he laughed and said he hadn't thought about that form in years. But Donna remembered it well, as one of Rick's first efforts to make something that couldn't be made in any other way. Rick recalled the mold as being primitive. "I hardly knew anything." He was frustrated by the "roundness" of thrown clay at the time. "No matter how you manipulate wet clay, it still has that genesis of roundness." Slip casting was a way to add a different dimension to his work. Rick wishes he'd continued with slip casting then, but it wasn't possible in his studio. He found it difficult to throw and make molds simultaneously, and he just wasn't finished with throwing yet, so he set slip casting aside for a while.

Rick never experienced the nega-

Donna Polseno

Untitled, 2006
4 x 13 x 7 inches (10.2 x 33 x 17.8 cm)
Slip cast; electric fired; multiple glazes using wax resist, cone 4
Photo by Tim Barnwell

tive public attitudes toward casting that other ceramists report having confronted back then. "No, that's why I think now I probably should have been more adventurous and taken that road earlier. Knowing what I know now, I would have been a lot happier person then! I think I just would have been freer to make things in various other shapes and other forms and not have to personally work so hard." His experience with casting during that period paved the way for he and Donna to think about casting as a medium years later.

Rick doesn't find casting as physically backbreaking as throwing pottery on a wheel. "In a weird way, it's kind of liberating because once you've taken responsibility for the forms, you don't have to think about them tomorrow." He appreciates not having to reinvent forms every day, the way he feels you do when you're at the wheel, and not having to wonder "Is it big enough? Is it wide enough? Is it tall enough? Should I add a little more clay? Should it be a little bit taller? You don't have to think about it; you did that thing; it's over with. Now comes the challenge of integrating glazes and textures and images onto that form in a new and fresh way."

Both Donna and Rick keep their slip-cast work fresh by regularly making new molds and by throwing out older ones. Rick doesn't believe

DONNA POLSENO graduated from the Kansas City Art Institute and in 1974 received her M.F.A. from the Rhode Island School of Design. Since that time she has been a studio artist living and working in the mountains of Virginia with her husband, Richard Hensley. Donna has made many kinds of ceramic pieces over the years, including slab-built raku baskets and boxes, abstract earthenware vessel forms, large figurative sculpture, slip-cast figurative vases, and functional pottery.

A recipient of two grants from the National Endowment for the Arts and a grant from the Virginia Museum of Fine Arts, Donna has taught workshops and summer sessions at many schools, including the Portland School of Art, Arrowmont School of Arts and Crafts, Alfred University, Penland School of Crafts, Rochester Institute of Technology, the University of Michigan, and the Jingdezhen Ceramic Institute in Jingdezhen, China. She has also been a resident at the Archie Bray Foundation and an invited participant in a ceramic symposium in Turkey. Her work is included in many prestigious permanent collections, such as the Federal Reserve Bank in Virginia, the Kansas City Art Institute, and the Mint Museum of Craft and Design in North Carolina. Donna now teaches part-time at Hollins University in Roanoke, Virginia.

Richard Hensley

Plant Form Bottle, 2002
15 x 7 x 4 inches (38.1 x 17.8 x 10.2 cm)
Assembled cast parts, stoneware; cone 10,
reduction
Photo by Tim Barnwell

that making molds is artistically limiting in and of itself. As he explains,
"If you're going to be a person who
gets locked in, you'll get locked in.
Molds themselves are not going to
keep you from looking around and
having new insights about yourself
and your work."

Rick and Donna have created more
than 175 series of forms, and their
way of working has changed quite a
bit in recent years. They used to go
through the six-step process of mak-

ing the clay prototype, the original
plaster master mold, the new plaster
prototype, the new mold, the master
mold, and the working mold. Now
they make molds that are much more
experimental and that are destined
for a much shorter casting life. These
molds may be in the shop for only a
few months before a new idea takes
hold and newer molds are made. "We
still make molds like crazy—especially
Donna—but most of the forms are
very singular and may have lives of
just a few months. The glazing and
decorating process has become para-
mount and takes quite a long time.
We aren't as production oriented now;
we just try to make a few runs of
each new idea—maybe 25 to 50. We
get really lucky with some of them,
and then move on, based on what
we've learned. Our molds now are
much simpler and never 'perfect.' We
aren't going to keep them that long

"For us, everything is a possibility to be explored and taken advantage of."

Richard Hensley

Plant Form Bottles, 2005
10 x 5 x 5 inches (25.4 x 12.7 x 12.7 cm)
Assembled cast parts, stoneware and porcelain; cone 10
Photo by Tim Barnwell

Richard Hensley

and will never need to reproduce them. For us, everything is a possibility to be explored and taken advantage of."

Coming up with fresh ideas hasn't been a problem for Donna or Rick. One idea generates another. Donna draws and keeps notebooks that she uses all the time. She often derives new ideas for cast work from her one-of-a-kind work; it's a back-and-forth process for her. Donna's inspiration for her first cast pieces came from her own large-scale, earthenware figurative sculpture. She created smaller, more stylized versions as vases that were slip cast. Over time her sculptures evolved; the figures she made were about women holding and presenting classical pottery forms. This led her to an interest in making more traditionally functional pottery, and she continues to find molds useful as tools for creating her work.

Clearly, Rick and Donna have demonstrated the curiosity, drive, and tenacity that it takes to be self-supporting artists. But even more important, they strive for a constant standard of excellence and beauty. That standard makes them two of the most admired potters working today.

Cast Teapot, 2004
6 x 9 x 4 inches (15.2 x 22.9 x 10.2 cm)
Assembled cast parts, pulled handle, porcelain; cone 10; strontium orange glaze
Photo by Tim Barnwell

RICHARD HENSLEY graduated in 1972 from the Kansas City Art Institute, where he studied with Ken Ferguson and Victor Babu. He received his M.F.A. from the Rhode Island School of Design. In 1974 Richard and his wife, Donna Polseno, moved to Floyd, a small town in the mountains of southwest Virginia, and he has been making pottery and various other clay objects ever since. He has taught workshops and given presentations at East Tennessee State University, Virginia Polytechnical University, Craft Alliance in Missouri, and other institutions throughout the United States. He has taught at Kent State University, Alfred University, and the Rochester Institute of Technology. Richard has also received a grant from the National Endowment for the Arts, made ceramics at the Archie Bray Foundation, taught a workshop in China, and worked in Turkey at an international ceramic symposium. He now teaches ceramics at Hollins University in Roanoke, Virginia.

Richard has concentrated on porcelain ceramics and has always complemented his wheel-thrown porcelain work with forms and ideas for molded objects. For many years he helped Donna with a long-running series of slip-cast vases and, after 10 years of that work, considers himself to be an expert mold maker.

slip formulation

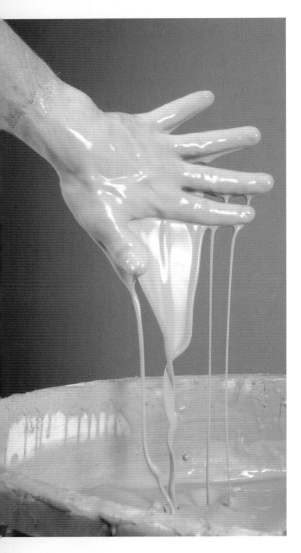

Casting slip is formulated in a way completely different from the plastic clays used for wheel throwing; its desired quality is nonplastic rather than plastic. This chapter is designed to help you understand how casting slip works; it includes descriptions of the types of clays used in slips and their properties, and instructions for making homemade slips. Slip recipes are provided in the Appendixes on page 151.

DEFLOCCULATION: THE KEY TO SLIP

A bag of commercial low-fire clay and a commercially mixed low-fire slip are very similar—sometimes identical—in composition (50 percent ball clay and 50 percent talc) and are also very similar in their percentages of water. How is this possible? The answer has to do with electricity.

Imagine two magnets, each of which has both a positive and negative charge. Any two particles of clay behave in exactly the same way as two magnets. A clay particle is plate shaped and octagonal. The edge of the plate has a positive charge, and the flat surface has a negative charge. In particles of plastic clay, as in magnets, the positive and negative charges are attracted to each other, and the plates are bound together by this electrical force. Clay particles literally flock together like sheep, resulting in what's known as *flocculated* clay.

The introduction of a *deflocculant,* such as sodium silicate or soda ash (a sec-

ondary deflocculant), changes the positive electrical charge on the edge of the clay plate to a negative charge. When this occurs, the plates repel each other, just as two similarly charged magnets do; the clay particles no longer flock—they deflock. Every clay particle repels every other clay particle because they all have the same electrical charge.

My early, uneducated attempts to slip cast bore a resemblance to early eighteenth-century European slip casting, in which water and clay were simply mixed together without deflocculants. To make this mixture liquid, extra water was added. As a result the slip would settle out, crack easily, and shrink much more than usual. The discovery of deflocculation in the mid-1800s, which eliminated high shrinkage and lowered loss rates, made the mass production of slip-cast wares a viable proposition.

The first slip I tried to mix was a stoneware throwing body. Like the early Europeans, I wasn't even aware that slip needed deflocculation. As a result, the castings never came out of the mold. Eventually I found out about sodium silicate, which is used as a deflocculant, and although adding it helped the stoneware slip work better to some degree, my slip was still a gooey mess. Next, I tried deflocculating porcelain throwing scraps. This slip worked better, but the bentonite in the clay retained too much water, leaving the castings very malleable. Soon after I was given Tom Spleth's casting-slip recipe (see page 151) and started to engage in serious slip casting. I've used this same basic casting slip, with some of my own modifications, for years.

TYPES OF SLIP-CASTING CLAY BODIES

Casting slip is a very particular type of clay that has to meet a different set of technical criteria than plastic bodies. In contrast to throwing bodies, casting-slip clay bodies are generally nonplastic, with a mix of 50 percent clay and 50 percent fillers and fluxes, and without any highly plastic elements such as bentonite. Most slip recipes stay close to this 50/50 ratio, although some of the recipes on page 151 do break this basic rule—and do produce casting slips that work well. Beyond this common element, casting slips can vary widely in their technical and aesthetic qualities, and you may have to develop your own particular slip to meet your aesthetic needs and technical demands.

Plaster is similar to a massive, rigid sponge filled with evenly sized pores; the size of the pores is determined by the consistency of the plaster. When plaster absorbs water from the slip through these pores, small capillaries transfer the water to the outside of the mold, where the water evaporates. If you were to look at casting-slip particles and the surface of plaster under a microscope, the clay particles would look much larger than the pores of the plaster. When casting slip is poured into a mold, the plaster absorbs water until the excess liquid slip is drained from the mold (as with a drain-cast mold) or until there's no water left to absorb (as with a solid-cast mold). At this point, the casting begins to shrink. Because the clay particles are larger than the pores, the clay will not embed itself in the plaster; instead, as the casting dries, it releases from the mold. This process depends on plaster of the correct consistency and on a casting body in which the water, clays, and clay *particle sizes* (these are measured in microns) are balanced correctly.

testing casting slip

In my experience and in industry, porcelain (or generally white) clay bodies are the most naturally well suited to slip casting. Some terra-cotta and stoneware bodies will cast well, but as a general rule, these types of bodies are more difficult because they contain a higher percentage of clay and include clays that are more plastic and hence retain more water. Usually these slips are difficult or impossible to defloccu-late because the clay is too plastic and retains water, or the iron in them has a retarding effect on the deflocculant. Some of these nonporcelain slips can be made liquid with deflocculant, but they don't have a sufficient *casting rate* and will gel too quickly.

There are two ways to determine whether a particular clay will defloccu-late easily. The first is to examine the clay's technical data sheet, provided by the manufacturer, to determine the percentage of the clay with a particle size of below 5 microns and the per-centage below .5 micron. This particle-size information will tell you how fine the microscopic particles are.

Take a look at the Comparing Clays chart on page 118. The higher the per-centage number in the "Below .5 Micron" column, the finer the particles. The finer the particles, the more water

Rebecca Harvey

Sink, 2004
7 x 5 x 5 inches (17.8 x 12.7 x 12.7 cm)
Press-molded and assembled porcelain; cone 6, oxidation
Photo by artist

the clay will retain and the more plastic it will be. The lower the number in that column, the coarser the clay particles. Coarse-particle clays will release water easily, so a lower number indicates a clay that's more desirable for formulating casting slip.

The second piece of data to review on the manufacturer's data sheet is the CEC/MBI number, also known as the *exchange rate*, which indicates how easily a clay will deflocculate. The lower the exchange rate number, the better. *Kaolins*—the primary clays in porcelain bodies—have the lowest numbers, with exchange rates of 1.2 to 5. They're followed by ball clays, with exchange rates of 5 to 10, and then iron-bearing clays (20 and higher). These numbers don't tell you how well a clay will cast—only how easily it will deflocculate.

Once you've read the technical data for the clay, a second way to determine its casting suitability is to mix a test batch, although usually the data sheet will be sufficient. To make a test batch, I mix 50 percent of the individual clay with 50 percent nonplastics (25 percent potash feldspar and 25 percent flint). From this test batch, you can learn about the individual qualities of the clay and how they will affect your casting slip.

comparing clays

	Below 5 Microns	Below .5 Micron	Exchange Rate
Ball Clays			
FC-120	73	39	8.5
FC-340	79	39	9.0
FC-400	79	50	10.0
S-3	77	37	8.5
S-4	84	45	9.6
F-2 (red earthenware)	74	22	22.0
C & C	84	54	9.0
Spinks Blend	76	42	7.0
Spinks Special	79	50	7.8
New Foundry Hill Crème	74	42	8.7
Tennessee #1 SPG	78	37	6.6
Martin #5	72	28	5.3
Martin #5 L-1 (blend)	70	28	5.9
L-1	68	30	6.8
Old Mine #4 (OM4)	86	43	10.1
Kaolins			
EPK	81	41	4.5
KT Cast	81	30	2.5
Grolleg	N/A	58	N/A
Velvacast	N/A	39	1.2

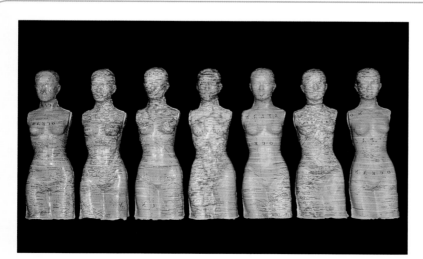

Paula Smith

Seven Women, 2006
10 x 24 x 2 inches (25.4 x 61 x 5 cm)
Slip-cast porcelain; mixed media; cone 6
Photo by artist

Ceramic engineers design and mix clay bodies using a variety of different clays. Part of the method they use, known as particle packing, is an effort to fit many different-sized clay particles together. Most potters who use plastic clay do the same by mixing several different clays in order to counteract the variations of any individual one. A variety of particle sizes is added to the clay recipe; the largest are those of feldspar and flint. In cast ware, where there's no compression from the forming process, the tighter the pack, the stronger the green ware.

At Kohler Company, castings are moved and handled many times prior to firing. They are even glazed while green. Their casting body is very tough in the green state, due largely to the fact that the clay content in the body is predominantly ball clay.

kaolins

Kaolins, also known as China clays, are the whitest firing of all clays and also the easiest to deflocculate for casting slip. Unlike ball clays, which are *secondary clays* (ones transported from their sources by natural forces such as the movement of water and erosion), kaolins are *primary clays* (ones that haven't been moved by erosion and therefore lack impurities).

grolleg english china clay

Grolleg is by far the best kaolin to use for high-fire and midrange porcelain casting slips. Because it consists of blended kaolin that's composed of 29 different clays, its particles are already varied in size. Unlike American kaolins, Grolleg is low in titanium dioxide, which makes clays nontranslucent. Another excellent English kaolin is Standard Porcelain, which is even better in casting slips than Grolleg. Many other kaolins can be tested for casting and throwing bodies. Grolleg tends to retain water but can be balanced with EPK and ball clays.

tile #6

Tile #6 was created to compete with Grolleg in the American market. In most throwing and casting instances, I consider it to be a poor man's substitute, not only because it's so much less expensive than Grolleg, but also because, in the tests I've made, it doesn't perform as well in the cast body. In addition, Tile #6 contains titanium dioxide, so it's less translucent than Grolleg. Like Grolleg, Tile #6 by itself in a test slip tends to retain water, so it must be balanced with EPK and ball clays.

epk

EPK acts to dry the casting and will counteract the tendency of Grolleg and Tile #6 to retain water. If you mix a casting slip with straight EPK, feldspar, and flint (in 50/25/25 proportions, respectively), the water in your casting slip will be absorbed very slowly because the particles in the slip are packed together so tightly that they inhibit the flow of water into the mold. As a result, the casting will develop only a very thin wall. It will also cake to the mold and will not release on its own. So, as a single clay casting body, EPK won't work.

velvacast

This clay is engineered for slip casting. Unlike most clays used for pottery, it is water washed rather than air floated. In the water-washing process, the slurry is sieved in a centrifuge to determine the average particle size of the clay. This kaolin has a coarse particle size that promotes rapid casting and mold release. Both Velvacast and KT Cast (see the next paragraph) are worth testing in small batches.

kt cast

Engineered specifically for slip casting, KT Cast is a nonplastic kaolin produced by Dry Branch Kaolin and has a lower exchange rate than any other kaolin. It's a good addition to a casting body, as it promotes fast casting and easy release from the mold.

Mathew S. McConnell

EASX050K0805A15, 2005
15 x 11 x 9 inches (38.1 x 27.9 x 22.9 cm)
Slip-cast and assembled earthenware; cone 05
Photo by artist

Chris Gustin

Alcobaca Vase #9934, 1999
20 x 9 x 8 inches (50.8 x 22.9 x 20.3 cm)
Slip-cast porcelain; wood fired in anagama kiln, cone 11
Photo by Dean Powell

comparing kaolins

Kaolins perform in widely different ways in casting slips, depending on the percentages of the combined clays. Following are some observations I've made during slip testing.

When mixed in a straight clay test with 50 percent clay, 25 percent potash feldspar, and 25 percent flint, both Grolleg and Tile #6 retain so much water that the casting is soft, remains gooey for a long time, and never really dries.

It's easy to see that neither the Grolleg/Tile #6 clays nor EPK will work well on their own. Together, however, they work to balance a slip formula. I have only peripheral experience with the other kaolins. As with all clays, test these in small batches to ensure that they'll work in your casting situation. The other component that helps determine how well the slip is absorbed and releases is ball clay.

ball clays

One of the most important considerations when calculating porcelain casting bodies is an understanding of ball clays. While there are few kaolins from which to choose, dozens of ball clays exist, all with different qualities and different influences on the slip. Ball clays, which complement kaolins, are secondary clays. In the process of moving from their original sites, ball clays pick up organic material, which makes them more plastic than kaolins. Often ball clay is found in stratified layers of coal. The largest deposits in the United States are in western Kentucky and Tennessee. The movement of the Mississippi River and of glaciers during the Ice Ages contributed to the formation of ball clay in these areas.

Spinks Blend and Tennessee #9 SGP are ball clays that are commonly available and very useful. They can be used together or by themselves with good results. All clay manufacturers provide brochures that indicate which of their ball clays are best suited for slip casting.

The one drawback to ball clays is that they contain from 1 to nearly 2 percent titanium and iron. The titanium imparts opacity to the body and diminishes its translucency; the iron makes the fired clay gray and buff in color. I test-fire clays to see their fired colors and to assess how they'll affect the color of the fired casting slip. Then I test the clay in a small batch of slip. If translucency is desired, I lower the percentage of ball clays in the recipe.

For more complicated forms with indentations, a slip with more ball clay will allow more stretching as the slip dries in the mold before the casting is released. If translucency and whiteness are unimportant, a body can be composed with a high percentage of ball clay, with EPK added to dry out the ball clay's plasticity.

The three primary ball-clay suppliers that cater to potters are H.C. Spinks Clay Company, Kentucky-Tennessee Clay Company, and Old Hickory Clay Company. Each produces ball clays suitable for slip casting. Spinks and KT also process a variety of kaolins. As with kaolins, the most important quality of a ball clay is its percentage of particles below 5 microns and below .5 micron, and its exchange rate, which is provided on the data sheets as CEC/MBI (see page 118).

To summarize, the finer the particles in a clay, the more water the slip will retain; the coarser the particles, the more easily the slip will release water. A lower exchange rate indicates that the clay deflocculates more easily.

fluxes

A flux melts the silica in the clay and vitrifies, or tightens, the clay body. Fluxes are required in casting slips in order for the clay to vitrify in the fire.

talc

Talc is used as a flux in low-fire bodies. Most low-fire commercial slips contain 50 percent ball clay and 50 percent talc. Occasionally talc is used in conjunction with small percentages of *frits* (see the next paragraph). One caution here: Using talc in clay bodies that are fired above cone 5 can result in *bloating* and severe slumping. Bloating, which occurs when a clay body is overfired, results in lumps on the surface of a pot; the clay looks almost as if it had boiled.

frits

Frits are used as a secondary flux in low-fire and midrange slips, along with talc in low-fire slips and feldspars in midrange slips. Often a boron flux is used because it has a lower melting temperature than feldspar. Frits tend to be expensive, so they're usually used in low percentages.

feldspar

The three basic types of feldspars are soda, potash, and lithium. I've found that soda feldspar as the sole flux in a casting body is slightly more difficult to deflocculate than potash feldspar, so it's best to combine soda and potash feldspars in midrange clay bodies. Small additions of lithium feldspar are beneficial to midrange casting slips. In general, lithium feldspars aren't used in casting slips because lithium feldspar is a very volatile flux and is more expensive than other fluxes. In high-fire slips, potash feldspar is used straight, or two potash feldspars are combined.

The most commonly available feldspars are potash feldspars (Custer, G-200, and K-200) and soda feldspars (nepheline syenite and Kona F-4). Check with your clay supplier to see if any local feldspars are available in your area; they may be less expensive.

fillers

Fillers are nonplastic and nonfluxing materials; each adds a particular quality to the clay body. To call a material a filler implies that its effects on the clay body are inconsequential. In practice, however, fillers do "fill" a critical proportion of the clay mixture, and each makes a contribution that differs from the contributions of the clay and fluxes.

flint

Flint (also known as quartz or silica) is the most common filler used in midrange and high-temperature bodies. Decreasing the fluxes and increasing the flint, however, can inhibit glass formation, making the clay less vitreous. To make a strong and balanced clay body, there must be a balance of clays, fluxes, and fillers. In extreme cases of high flint and low fluxes, the clay will fail to bond during firing and, when it cools, may shatter (a process known as *dunting*). Within a normal range, however, you can adjust your glaze by adding flint to the body. Adding flint will help prevent *crazing,* a condition in which the glaze fits too tightly and cracks during glaze firing. Crazing may be desirable in some cases, but in extreme cases, the glaze compresses the body so severely that it makes the clay weak.

alumina

In industry, *alumina* is used to raise the firing temperature of clay bodies in order to inhibit slumping and increase the fired strength. A *refractory* material (one resistant to melting), alumina is used in casting slips to perform the same function. Alumina eliminates translucency in the clay body. It is usually substituted in equal parts for flint, up to 10 percent. Hotel china bodies usually include up to 10 percent alumina. Like *pyrophyllite* (see page 122), alumina is expensive, but even 2 percent will add substantial strength to your clay. If the clay will be salt or soda glazed, alumina will repel the sodium vapor, resulting in a dry surface rather than a glazed surface. This fact can be used for decorative purposes; adding

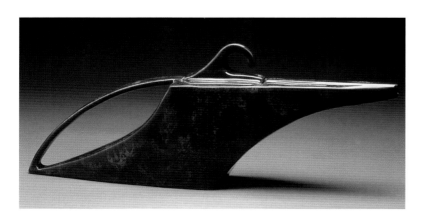

Charles B. Nalle

Blue Racer Teapot, 2004
6 x 14 x 4 inches (15.2 x 35.6 x 10.2 cm)
Three-piece mold cast; dipped and exterior sprayed; single fired, cone 6
Photo by David Coulter

an alumina slip will provide a matte finish that contrasts with a glazed area imparted by salt or soda.

pyrophyllite

This is an alumina silicate, with no fluxes and no plasticity, and is roughly analogous to calcined kaolin. It is used instead of flint as a filler in porcelain bodies and is generally assumed to add strength to them, although tests on similar clay bodies with and without pyrophyllite do not prove this contention. The popular Cornell throwing body includes pyrophyllite, supposedly to give strength to the body generally and in oven use. In the pots I've seen used in this manner, bodies without pyrophyllite actually wear better and crack less. Usually it replaces flint in the body; this often causes the glaze on the fired piece to craze substantially more than a glaze on the same body without pyrophyllite. Using pyrophyllite as a filler is also much more expensive than using flint.

defloculants

Deflocculants have properties that are useful in a variety of situations and conditions. Some commercial slipware manufacturers mix various deflocculants so that their slip is as elastic as possible. I use just sodium silicate because I want my slip to be as fluid as possible. Through trial and error you will find a single deflocculant—or blend of them—that will suit your casting slip and your forms.

sodium silicate

Sodium silicate is the most widely used deflocculant for casting slips and is added to the slip as a percentage by weight. As with all deflocculants, begin with .25 percent and increase the percentage up to .5 percent. If a slip is overdeflocculated, a skin will develop on the wet surface, both in the bucket and while casting (see page 134). In cases of severe overdeflocculation, the slip will be liquid for a short period and then gel.

soda ash

Traditionally, a small percentage of soda ash is dissolved and added to slip, along with sodium silicate, as a secondary deflocculant. Soda ash makes the casting more elastic—a useful function with forms that are very elaborate and need to stretch in the mold after draining and prior to release. Soda ash is very caustic, and even a little of it will speed up the rate of mold deterioration. As with all deflocculants, too much soda ash will cause the slip to gel.

darvan #7

Darvan #7 is a common deflocculant and is used in place of sodium silicate and soda ash. It is also sodium based. It's a popular slip deflocculant, but the manufacturer, R.T. Vanderbilt, recommends it as a glaze deflocculant. Darvan #7 was developed in the late 1950s and has since been replaced as a clay deflocculant by Darvan #811.

darvan #811

This deflocculant was developed in the late 1980s and is more sophisticated and powerful than Darvan #7. Consequently, it takes as little as .13 percent to deflocculate a batch of slip. Darvan #811 is recommended as a deflocculant for high-iron slip, with the addition of barium to increase the casting rate. R.T. Vanderbilt has formulated this deflocculant to work even when a batch of slip is mixed from 100 percent dry casting scrap.

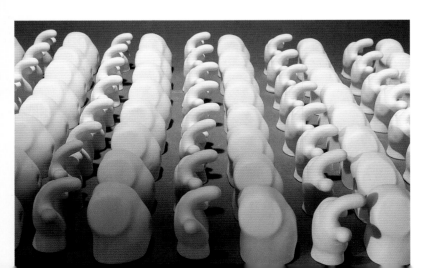

Sue Kay Lee

To a New World Order, 2005
3 x 36 x 25 inches (7.6 x 91.4 x 63.5 cm)
Molded and cast white-ware slip; cone 04
Photo by artist

water

Water, like clay and feldspar, is a mixture of various chemicals. Some waters are hard, some are soft, some taste better than others, and some are undrinkable. The same type of water that is beneficial to throwing bodies—water that is high in organic material content and low in mineral content—benefits casting slip as well. The School of Ceramic Engineering at Alfred University uses deionized water (water with the minerals removed and the organic material left in) for mixing test slips. In practice, deionizers are too costly for studio potters, but I found an affordable one while watching an infomercial—and it works! It attaches to a garden hose and is marketed as a means of providing spot-free rinses for cars and windows. (The rinses are spot free because there aren't any minerals in the water.)

While Tom Spleth was at Alfred, he noticed that the slip at school deflocculated differently than it did at his studio. The difference was that the school's tap water was very hard; at his studio, Tom was using nonpotable pond water that was full of rotted organic material and therefore more beneficial to deflocculation of his casting slip.

When I first set up my studio, I wanted pond water with which to mix casting slip. I was in an urban area with no nearby ponds, however, so I simulated pond water by throwing grass clippings into a 30-gallon (113.6 L) barrel of water. The result of this endeavor was a studio filled with the ripe smell of compost! The solution was to wash all the casting equipment in a 30-gallon (113.6 L) trash can. Because clay is full of organic material that benefits plastic clay as it ages, when the residual clay from the casting equipment soaked in this "rotting pond," the water became excellent for mixing casting slip.

SLIP-MIXING EQUIPMENT

The best tool for mixing casting slip is a homemade or manufactured blunger. A good mixer should have a fan-cooled motor, a 1-inch-diameter (2.5 cm) stainless-steel shaft, and a propeller large enough to mix the volume of slip in the bucket completely. The propeller should be mounted at a 15-degree angle so that the slip doesn't form a whirlpool during mixing, and the turning speed should be slow to medium, not fast.

I built a relatively inexpensive blunger that's worked well for years. The motor is geared down from 1750 rpm to 300 rpm by means of belts and pulleys. When mixing slip, the motor turns very slowly, and the final ingredients have to be forced into the mix with a boat oar. If you mix slip at a high speed, you don't have to mix as long. If you mix the slip for a long period at high speed, the friction of the clay particles against each other will raise the slip from room temperature to as high as 110°F (43.3°C). This probably won't hurt the casting slip, but it does cause the water to evaporate, and the slip has to cool before it's used.

The one change I'd make to my blunger is to its pulley system. I'd replace the one pulley on each shaft with a pulley that had three adjustments so that I could move the belt between the pulleys when I wanted to change the mixing speed. This would allow me to switch between high-speed mixing at the beginning and low-speed mixing once the powders were absorbed by the liquid.

Ginny Conrow

Night Sky Envelope Vase, 2006
11 x 6 x 3 inches (27.9 x 15.2 x 7.6 cm)
Porcelain slip; crystalline glaze, electric fired, cone 10
Photo by Roger Schreiber

Amy M. Santoferraro

Doe Post, 2006
12 x 8 x 8 inches (30.5 x 20.3 x 20.3 cm)
Slip-cast porcelain; electric fired, cone 6; felt
Photo by artist

MIXING SLIP

You may want to mix a test batch of slip to see how it works. To make about 10 gallons (37.9 l) of slip, you'd need about 100 pounds (45.4 kg) of dry clay. To make the test batch, you'll need 100 pounds (4.54 kg) of dry, mixed clay, with 40 percent water and .25 percent of sodium silicate or Darvan #7. (The water and sodium silicate are calculated as a percentage of the dry mix total.) Sodium silicate is calculated in grams because the tolerance between correct deflocculation and over-deflocculation can be very exacting.

Begin with the water and .25 percent of sodium silicate. (The acceptable range of deflocculant is .25 to .5 percent.) Then add the clays, and mix until smooth. Now add the feldspar and flint, and mix again until smooth. Use a very small mixing blade and try not to create a whirlpool, which will suck air into the mixture.

Let the slip rest overnight. The next day, mix the slip again and pour it through a screen somewhat finer than window screen—about 30 mesh. Because the quantities of water and clay are known and constant, the variable that enables you to adjust the fluidity of the slip is the amount of sodium silicate. At this stage, the slip will be just about the right thickness (slightly thick).

mixing wet & dry scraps

You'll inevitably end up with casting scraps and broken greenware. When mixing new slip, you can add up to 25 percent dry scrap and the appropriate amount of water to the blunger barrel before mixing. Take a look at the slip recipes on pages 151; they'll help you understand the following example:

If you were mixing 300 pounds (136 kg) of new slip, you'd start with 120 pounds (56.7 kg) of water—40 percent of 300 pounds (136 kg). If you wanted to include dry scrap, you could add up to 75 pounds (34 kg) of it—25 percent of the total. You'd also need to add another 30 pounds (13.6 kg) of water to the 120 pounds (56.7 kg) required by the slip recipe—40 percent of the added scrap.

If you choose to do this, start out by adding the 75 pounds (34 kg) of scrap to the total amount of water required—150 pounds (68 kg). Let the scraps soak for one hour. Then add the deflocculant and the dry ingredients required to make the new 300-pound (136 kg) batch of slip. Scrap contains sodium silicate already, so you'll make any necessary adjustments when you make final adjustments after mixing the slip and letting it rest overnight. All kinds of junk gets into the scrap, but don't worry; you'll screen it out before casting (see page 130 and 132).

mixing a large batch of slip

Mixing a large batch (100 to 400 pounds or 45.4 kg to 181.4 kg) of casting slip is quite easy if you have a blunger. If you don't, mixing with a drill can be a tedious job. For large batches, a very strong drill with a large propeller is definitely required.

To mix a large batch, first write down the recipe ingredients, multiplying the dry materials, water, and deflocculant as necessary. (Check each material off as you add it to the mix.) Weigh the water and add it to the mixing bucket (see photo 1). Add .25 percent deflocculant (.1 percent if you're using Darvan #811). If you have clay scraps, add them next, and let them soak for an hour (see photo 2). Then add the clays and mix until smooth (see photo 3). Add the non-plastics next, stirring these materials in if they don't mix in easily.

Pouring weighed water into the mixing barrel for a 400-pound (181.4 kg) batch of slip

Added dried scrap to the barrel

Adding clays to the mixture

When making a large batch of slip, I let it mix for up to 12 hours, or overnight. This lengthy period gives the fine particles of clay time to shear down, and the turning slip carries up to the surface all the small air bubbles that were introduced in the powders. If this air isn't eliminated, you'll see very fine bumps on the interior of the casting. Air bubbles trapped in the slip will often show through the glaze, so eliminating them during mixing is essential. I've had these bubbles bloat in refired pots, expanding to as large as golf balls.

After checking the specific gravity and viscosity by feel and by eye, or with instruments, and adjusting with a 50/50 mixture of deflocculant and water, you will be ready to proceed with casting.

specific gravity & viscosity

The specific gravity of slip is the ratio of the density (weight) of the slip to an equal volume of water. For example, 100 cc of water weighs 100 grams. When 100 cc of slip is weighed, it should weigh between 165 grams and 180 grams; the specific gravity is said to be between 1.65 and 1.80. Although you may want to check the specific gravity with a hydrometer, this instrument does not accurately measure the specific gravity of deflocculated slip.

If the specific gravity (by weight) is high, add more water to decrease it, and remix the slip. You may use this remixed slip right away. If the specific gravity is too low, add a bit more dry clay, remix the slip until the added clay is incorporated, and wait a couple of hours before retesting the specific gravity.

The viscosity of a slip represents its ability (or inability) to flow freely. You can test viscosity by eye and feel, or

Lea Tyler

The Twins, 2006
7 x 3 x 4 inches (17.8 x 7.6 x 10.2 cm)
Slip-cast and assembled parts; electric fired, cone 6, oxidation; mother-of-pearl luster
Photo by artist

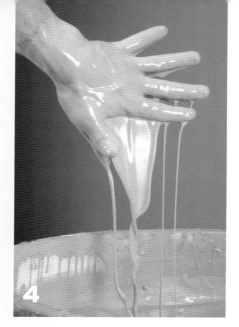

Holding my hand thumb-down and watching the viscosity of the slip

Waiting until the skin of my knuckles is exposed

Making a fist to see how much residual clay remains on my hand

with a viscosimeter. Slip that is too viscous flows out of the mold slowly, leaving residual slip in the mold, so the casting will take longer to dry before it can be removed from the mold. If the slip is the right viscosity, it flows easily from the mold, leaving very little residue, and the casting releases from the mold more quickly.

I leave the slip in my tumbler molds for 6 to 10 minutes, drain them, and remove them from the molds 20 minutes later. In a normal day I can cast these molds about 10 times because I use a low-viscosity slip—what I call "fast" slip.

To be perfectly honest, I've never used a viscosimeter; I test slip by eye and hand. First I mix the slip for about 12 hours, then let it rest for a day. The next day, after making sure the slip is well mixed, I turn off the blunger, dip my hand into the slip, and hold my hand with my thumb pointed down, so that the slip runs from one finger to the next (see photo 4).

I watch the speed at which the small particles of clay travel in the flowing slip. Slow-moving slip will be very apparent. I wait for about 10 seconds, until the skin of my knuckles is exposed (see photo 5). Then I squeeze my hand into a fist and watch to see how much slip is released (see photo 6). There should be very little. If the slip passes this visual test, it is fast slip; it will leave very little residue when it flows out of the mold.

If the slip is too thick, the skin of my knuckles isn't exposed as quickly, and when I squeeze my hand into a fist, a fair amount of residue is released. To thin the slip, use a squeeze bottle to add a mixture of 50 percent sodium silicate and 50 percent water, a few drops to a few teaspoons at a time mixing them in until they're thoroughly incorporated. Check the slip and continue to adjust it until it reaches the desired viscosity. While some potters prefer a thicker casting slip, I find that a thinner one allows for easy release of the air bubbles from the clay during mixing and facilitates easy draining from the mold during casting. I run

the specific gravity at 1.65 (more water), which decreases the time I spend holding an inverted mold during draining and thus speeds up my production process.

You can also test viscosity using a viscosimeter, which consists of a laboratory beaker with a rubber stopper and two tubes. One tube lets the slip out and one lets air into the beaker. Fill the beaker with 400 milliliters of freshly mixed slip. Then invert the beaker and watch the slip run out, measuring how long it takes until you see a break in the flow. If the break takes more than one minute to appear, add more sodium silicate and retest.

As you can see from this description, when you use a viscosimeter, you watch the slip carefully. Over time you'll begin to develop your own tactile and intuitive sense about the correct viscosity. I suggest starting with the tactile method and buying a viscosimeter only if necessary. In the meantime, save your money to buy something more important.

Richard Notkin
evolution is not an option—it's essential

20th Century Solutions Teapot: Nobody Knows Why (Yixing Series), 2003
9 ³/₈ x 15 ⁷/₈ x 11 inches (23.8 x 40.3 x 27.9 cm)
Slip-cast stoneware and hand-built elements; air-brushed engobe; electric fired, cone 5, oxidation
Photo by artist

When Richard was a ceramics major during the late 1960s, very few schools in the United States taught much about plaster, beyond telling students to add plaster to water and not the other way around. However, Richard studied with Ken Ferguson, who was wise enough to take him down to a local green-ware shop for a day. On the way there, Ken said, "Notkin, you've got the ideas; these people have the techniques." Richard has always appreciated that. "He wasn't worried that I was going to start slip casting frogs on lily pads. He knew I was going to do something else with my art. But he also knew that I needed to learn what those people could pass on. That was kind of the beginning of it all."

When Richard first started mold making and slip casting, all of his molds were based on found objects. He made a lot of these and combined the castings in sculptural pieces. Within a year or so, he started to feel as if his technical skills as a mold maker were dominating his aesthetic sensibility. His unique artistic person-ality—the so-called "sculptor's thumb"—was beginning to get lost.

By the time he entered graduate school in 1971, Richard had already begun fabricating molds from his own images sculpted in clay. Generating those images gave him some sense of regained control over his aesthetic sensibility. He also developed a fasci-nation with alteration of scale. Some of the pieces he casts (his *Curbside*

Teapot series is a good example) are fairly realistic but are literally shrunk to about one-twelfth of their actual size. All the realistic, but diminutive, tree trunks, fire hydrants, and dogs in these pieces are objects for which Richard carved the originals. "If I worked on a one-to-one scale, I would simply make molds of already existing objects. But I love to carve and to alter realism, and I often employ sur-realistic devices, including the manip-ulation of scale."

He tries to alter each casting in a way that will create a unique object; he has no interest in creating the same piece over and over again. "The fine-arts market to which I'm appeal-ing is one that desires unique, as opposed to mass-produced, objects." Each of his sculptural teapots has about a dozen separate castings on average, and some contain as many as two or three hundred separately cast elements that are uniquely combined, and/or altered and combined. Each object takes Richard at least one full week to make; some of the more com-plex pieces require a month or more. "People often think of molds as ves-sels from which you can make a hun-dred identical objects a day, and that's a valid part of the process. But my approach to making unique objects is this: if I'm going to take a week to make a teapot, why should I take another week to make that same teapot, when I could make and explore a different combination of elements and make a new teapot instead?"

In 1981 Richard shared a studio at the Archie Bray Foundation with Cary

Esser, who loaned him a copy of an exhibition catalog of Yixing ware. Richard loved the pieces and began working on his Yixing teapot series in the early 1980s. He was determined to find a way to adapt slip casting (which is actually foreign to the making of real Yixing teapots) to create his own versions. In the making of Yixing pots, slip casting is taboo in China, Richard explains, as is using a potter's wheel. Yixing teapots are hand built, although press molds are also used. Most are constructed using template-cut slabs assembled into a vessel form, which is then placed inside a mold. This preassembled vessel is then pressed from within against the interior surface of the mold, refining the form and adding details. For most of the next 13 to 14 years, Richard created approximately 250 Yixing-inspired teapots.

In addition to the obvious time-saving aspects of replicating a complex image by using molds, Richard believes that another of the advantages is that a slip-cast vessel is quite structurally sound. Unlike plastic clay, deflocculated slip has no memory. Therefore, there are no tensions or stresses to cause warping or cracking, and an artist can achieve vessels and various hollow sculptural forms that are much lighter than hand-built forms, and that survive the kiln with virtually no cracking. Slip-cast forms can also be easily manipulated, altered, and combined with other slip-cast forms.

As his first venture into slip casting was during the hippie era of the late 1960s and early 1970s, Richard admits, with some embarrassment, that he mass-produced pipes— hundreds of them. "This was strictly

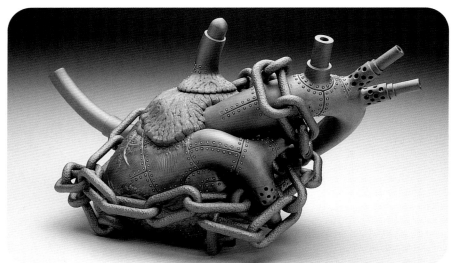

Heart Teapot: Hostage/Metamorphosis III (Yixing Series), 2004
6 ½ x 12 ¼ x 6 inches (16.5 x 31.1 x 15.2 cm)
Slip-cast stoneware parts, altered and combined; electric fired, cone 5, oxidation; two luster firings, cone 019
Photo by artist

a commercial venture; I put myself through graduate school making the damned things. I'd get up every morning and cast all 12 of my molds, have them cleaned by lunchtime, recast later in the afternoon, and work into the night. I'd make 24 pipes every day. Although I introduced a couple of new designs each year, ultimately, the

replication got boring, and I burned out. I felt like a human factory."

Richard believes that artists should be lifelong students but acknowledges that change can be difficult. "When you're designing new aesthetic images and making new prototypes and molds, the production of marketable work comes to a temporary halt. You must keep your mind focused on the goals for your work, and, if it's evolving and growing in positive ways, you will also be able to expand your market or your customer base." What is most important, Richard insists, both in a commercial sense and from a personal

ize that concept into an artwork. In the rarefied environment of the academic petri dish, the notions of 'truth to materials' and 'the nature of clay' have been repeated so often that they've taken on the aura of religious mantras. In actuality, these twin notions are little more than doctrines

gories and subcategories that comprise contemporary ceramic art: functional, sculptural, figurative, narrative, abstract, mixed media, conceptual and/or new genres, and more. Slip casting has indeed transcended its past associations with commercial mass production, and hobby and kitsch ceramics. This fact provides a strong argument that slip casting is simply another viable technique—another tool that enables artists to express their inner visions and passions—and is no better or worse than any other process. "If the technique is appropriate to actualizing your original concept, use it!"

"If the technique is appropriate to actualizing your original concept, use it"

standpoint, is renewing your artistic vigor, keeping your interest going, and keeping yourself from burning out. In his view, evolution isn't optional; it's an integral part of being an artist.

As Richard points out, slip casting has long been associated with mass-produced ceramic objects, ranging from early-twentieth-century Art Deco vases to toilets, salt-and-pepper shakers, 1950s ashtrays, and black and chartreuse jaguar lamps. In the latter half of the twentieth century, slip casting attained a popular hobby status, reflected by a plethora of green-ware shops churning out endless variations of glaze-it-yourself cookie jars and Santa Claus mugs.

"Relegated to a lowly pedestrian status and unfairly criticized by many academics and art critics, slip casting has too often been assigned-by an ersatz value scale that reeks of dogma and didactic nonsense-to the bottom rung of the ceramic arts technical hierarchy. Aesthetic value isn't determined by any supposed hierarchy of techniques, but by the unique relationship of the conceptual and intellectual intentions of the artist to the techniques, materials, scale, and imagery chosen to actual-

that elevate and promote certain techniques and processes while chastising and discouraging others. This dogmatic approach inevitably produces the types of prejudices that artificially favor and elevate certain techniques, processes, and philosophical approaches and denigrate all others. But in the final analysis, perhaps the late Pete Voulkos said it best: 'Technique is nothing if you have nothing to say with it.'"

Today, Richard says, the aesthetic aspects of ceramic art produced through the technique of slip casting encompass the full range of cate-

As an artist with more than 38 years of experience in mold making and slip casting, Richard has developed an approach that is initially cautious. "Be extremely critical of your prototype model before you produce the mold. The replication of an aesthetically bad idea is merely a bad idea multiplied; sheer quantity of objects won't obscure the dubious quality of the original concept."

RICHARD NOTKIN received his B.F.A. from the Kansas City Art Institute in 1970, and his M.F.A, from the University of California, Davis, in 1973. He has received numerous grants and fellowships, including the John Simon Guggenheim Memorial Foundation Fellowship in Sculpture in 1990 and the Louis Comfort Tiffany Foundation Fellowship in 1991; he also has been a three-time recipient of the National Endowment for the Arts Visual Artist Fellowship. His work has been included in many public collections—the Los Angeles County Museum of Art; the National Collection of Fine Arts (now the Smithsonian American Art Museum), Smithsonian Institution, Washington, D.C.; the Metropolitan Museum of Art; and the Victoria and Albert Museum, London, are just a few.

Richard is well known for his work with teapots, particularly his reinterpretation of the Yixing teapot. In recent years he has also created purely sculptural, nonfunctional pieces such as tile murals. Social/political commentary is inherent in much of his work.

casting

casting

The mold is made and the casting slip is mixed. Now it's time to reap the rewards of slip casting. The casting process is a bit like running a busy restaurant kitchen. Many things are happening simultaneously and in quick succession, so before casting, you must make sure that the casting slip, the molds, and your equipment are ready. Adequate preparation is the key to a smooth process.

PREPARING THE SLIP

At this point, you've mixed your slip, using one of two methods. Either you've mixed it with a blunger for 12 hours or you've mixed it periodically with a drill until it's free of lumps, then allowed it to rest for two to three days. In either case, you must test the viscosity of the slip just before casting (see page 125–126) and adjust it as necessary.

When you remove the slip from the mixing barrel, you must screen it before pouring it into the molds. Though the slip may look beautifully smooth, it will always contain bits of plaster, wood chips, and other junk that resides in recycled scrap. If you plan to pour only a few molds, a stainless-steel kitchen sieve will work. If you're planning a larger production, take the time to make a sieve. To do this, cut the bottom out of a 5-gallon (18.9 L) bucket, then cut the bucket in half between its rim and bottom. With duct tape, fasten a stainless-steel or bronze screen to the bottom of the lower section. Slide this portion of the bucket into the upper section to make a sieve. Then fit this sieve into another 5-gallon (18.9 L) bucket. Cover the slip until you're ready to use it.

Prepare one or more receptacles to receive the slip when you drain it from the molds. (Prior to casting, all the containers that will hold slip should be thoroughly cleaned of leftover slip or residue.) Unless you have a very strong back, place the receptacles on a bench or on stools so that you don't have to lift them from ground level. Ideally, receptacles for drained slip should have wheels on them so that you can move them up and down the casting line easily. I've always used a restaurant bus tub, about 16 x 24 inches (40.6 x 61 cm); it provides a wide target for the slip. Making a wheeled cart for the tub from 2 x 4 (3.8 x 8.9 cm) scraps is easy.

PREPARING THE MOLDS

Once the slip is ready and your sieve and draining receptacles are prepared, you can begin to prepare both new and old molds for the casting process. Bone-dry molds act like dry sponges, so they don't cast well; dampening them slightly activates the process of capillary attraction. You can introduce water to a mold in one of two ways. Dip the mold in a large tub of water (see photo 1). If the mold is too large, wipe the casting surface liberally with a fully saturated sponge (see photo 2). Disassemble large, multiple-piece molds before wetting them.

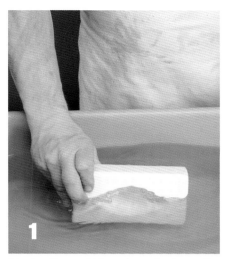

1

Dipping the mold in water prior to casting

2

Sponging a large mold to wet it

After wetting them, assemble and band multiple-piece molds for casting (see photo 3). Molds that split vertically are the most likely to leak. The taller a mold is, the greater the pressure that the slip will exert inside it, so your banding should be tight. For large molds, nylon belts, available from ceramic suppliers, or the metal banding used in shipping rooms are excellent. I use rubber bands for smaller molds (see photo 4). With large molds, I push wooden wedges under the belts to tighten them even further. Extra insurance always pays when casting.

Once, early on in my mold-making experience, I made some tall molds that each held about 6 gallons (22.7 L) of slip. They were split side to side, and my bands stretched too much to hold them together tightly. I severely under-estimated the amount of pressure the slip would exert. As I poured the slip into the first mold, just before it reached the top I thought that the mold was drinking up the slip very quickly. The mold seemed bottom-less—and it was! I finally saw that the pressure of the slip had pushed the mold apart, and the slip was pouring onto the floor. This is the slip-casting

version of the "Plaster Disaster" described on page 146.

Set the molds on a level surface, with enough room around each to allow you to pick it up when you drain it (see photo 5). As you arrange the casting line, group the molds by type and size. Casting times vary greatly. Handles that are solid cast take 10 to 25 minutes to absorb, but very thin cups can be cast in about five minutes. Place the molds that will cast quickly, such as small molds or handles, at the beginning of the casting line so that you can attend to them first as you move up the line. A line arrange-ment that suits you will become obvious after a few rounds of casting.

Inevitably, the table or the molds—or both—will need leveling. Prior to cast-ing, make many long, thin wedges to shim the molds to level. You can either position these near the molds prior to casting or carry a small bucket filled with them, and position them as you move down the line to fill the molds.

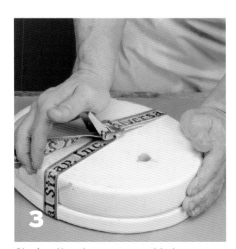

3

Closing the clamp on a mold strap

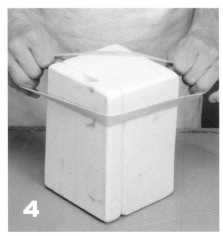

4

Putting a rubber band around a small mold

5

Molds ready for casting

CASTING

Learning how to cast molds is as much an art as a science. The steps appear to be straightforward. At the simplest level, you pour the slip into the mold, let it absorb to the desired thickness, then pour out the excess slip. Because there are a large number of parameters in casting that must be considered, the only way to figure out how to cast molds is to do it.

sieving the slip

Start by sieving slip into a 5-gallon (18.9 L) bucket (see photo 6). (Two buckets are usually sufficient for large casting operations.) If you have a slip

Sieving the slip

pump, you can sieve the slip through a screen and allow it to run back into the tank. Sieving will eliminate any lumps or residual wood and plaster chips. You can also pump through a sieve and into buckets.

Transfer the sieved slip to a 10-quart (9.5 L) spouted bucket. You'll use this bucket for pouring; keep it covered when it's not in use. (For smaller molds, you can transfer the slip into smaller pouring containers.) For filling very small molds and feeding molds with reservoirs, fill squeeze bottles with slip.

filling the molds

Filling molds is faster than emptying them, so staggering the process by filling only a few molds at a time eliminates the rush to empty them before the castings get too thick. When I cast dinnerware, for example, I fill four plate molds, wait five minutes, and then fill four more. Then, after five more minutes, I fill the last four. By the time I've filled the last four molds-or even before-the first molds are ready to be emptied. It takes me two minutes to empty the first four and suction up all the excess slip with a squeeze bottle. Then I wait a minute or two and move on to the next four.

Begin casting by filling the smallest molds—the ones that will have to be drained first (see photo 7). Fill the largest molds last (see photo 8). Always try to fill molds right up to the top edge without stopping. As you'll discover soon enough, if you stop partway through, a visible line will always be left at that point in the casting. This line doesn't present a structural problem, but it's unsightly; you'll need to sponge it off during cleanup.

As you fill the molds, you may find that some aren't level. Use wooden shims to prop up the bottom of any that aren't, under the area where the slip is closest to the rim. Push the shim under the mold until the slip appears level all the way around the rim, adding more shims if necessary (see photo 9). Finish filling the mold all the way to the top.

Check the thickness of the casting periodically by gently blowing the slip away from the mold at the edge of the casting (see photo 10). The longer the slip sits, the thicker the casting becomes. The optimum thickness of any given form is something you will arrive at by trial and error. As you cast, you'll make this decision based primarily on intuition and experience.

Wes Harvey

Sex Bears, 2006
5 x 12 x 7 inches (12.7 x 30.5 x 17.8 cm)
Slip-cast porcelain; low-fire glaze with luster; electric fired, cones 06 and 017
Photo by artist

Filling a small mold with a squeeze bottle

8

Filling a large mold with a bucket

9

Leveling a mold with a shim

For example, when I cast cups and saucers, once in a while my cups are too thick. Because I've allowed the slip to sit in the molds too long, the cups are just a tiny bit thicker and noticeably heavier, and their interiors have become smaller.

Because timing is the key to much of the casting process, an electronic kitchen timer is essential. While making molds, for example, I sometimes also cast tumblers. By using a timer to let me know me when to empty the molds, I can work on all the tasks involved in mold making and simultaneously cast up to 100 tumblers without giving them much thought.

10

Checking the thickness of a casting

David Pier

Pitcher #3 with Stacking Cups, 2003
Pitcher: 9 x 8 x 10 inches (22.9 x 20.3 x 25.4 cm);
cups: 4 x 4 x 4 inches (10.2 x 10.2 x 10.2 cm)
Porcelain slip; electric fired, cone 10, oxidation
Photo by artist

solving the problem of slip scum

As the slip sits in the mold, you may notice scum developing on its liquid surface. You can tell if you have this problem by dragging your index finger across the top of the slip (see photo 11). If a skin is forming, it will be noticeable. (You can't perform this test if the mold has a very small pour hole, of course, but scum usually develops only on molds that are large and open.)

This is a condition caused by too much deflocculant. As a consequence, when the slip is exposed to air as it rests in the mold or bucket, a skin forms on it. When you drain the mold, the slip will drain out from under the skin and some of the skin will be deposited on the interior surface of the casting. If this occurs, sponge the deposited clay off the casting before firing, as it will be noticeable under a transparent glaze.

A quick and easy solution to this problem is to spray the surface of the slip with water while the slip rests in the mold. This coating of water will prevent the skin from forming. Some people advocate countering this problem by reflocculating the slip with vinegar or barium. As long as my slip works well in every other way, I avoid trying to reverse the deflocculation. Allowing

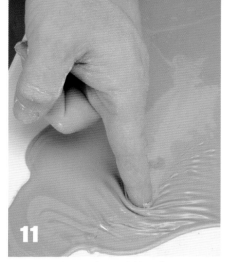

11

Scum on the surface of the slip

the casting slip to age a few days before pouring it into the molds will often eliminate the problem.

solid casting & drain casting

For solid-cast forms, clamp the mold together with two C-clamps or with a mold belt, place funnels in the tubes, and pour slip into one funnel. The slip will fill the cavity, pushing the air out through the other funnel and filling that second funnel partway as well (see photo 12).

The casting time, again, is based on experience, but using an electronic timer will help. Also, you can cast a small open mold at the same time; it will act as a visual guide to the thickness of the casting in the enclosed mold.

12

Filling a hollow-cast form with slip

To remove the slip-filled funnels, either put the butt end of a fettling knife in each one to plug the hole and then lift the funnel and knife out together, or just pull the funnel out quickly. If slip flows up out of the hole after you remove one funnel, the slip in the middle of the mold is still liquid. If it is, replace the funnel, remove the fettling knife, and repeat the process in a few minutes.

In some respects, casting hollow forms with molds consisting of more than one piece is similar to solid casting. You can't see the thickness of the casting as it builds up. Again, a small open mold cast at the same time will act as a guide to the thickness of the casting in the enclosed mold.

One other tip for casting hollow-cast molds: Tilt the mold so that the fill hole is slightly lower than the other hole. This will allow air to flow out of the mold as the slip fills it.

Vladimir Groh & Yasuyo Nishida

Teapot, 2006
5 x 9 x 6 inches (12.7 x 22.9 x 15.2 cm)
Slip-cast porcelain; gas fired, patina overglaze
Photo by Vladimir Groh

draining the molds

Pour the slip out of the mold and into a tub or barrel when the desired thickness has been reached (see photo 13). Sometimes, if molds are left to drain upside down, as the slip runs out, it will leave a ridgelike line on the interior of the casting. On a casting such as a plate and bowl, a line is definitely a visual detriment. To avoid creating this line, pour most of the slip out of the mold, keeping the mold tilted at an angle so that the residual slip drains into the corner where the floor meets the wall. Then use a turkey baster or a squeeze bottle with a large opening in its tip to suction up the excess slip that continues to flow off the walls and floor, leaving a little slip in the bottom of the mold (see photo 14). With flat-bottomed forms, turn the mold in the opposite direction, so the slip flows back across the whole floor of the casting (see photo 15). Return the mold to a vertical position on the table. The small amount of slip that remains on the floor of the mold will absorb in a short while.

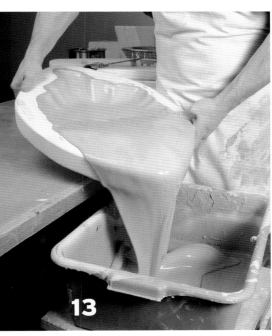

13

Draining the slip into a tub

14

Vacuuming residual slip with a squeeze bottle

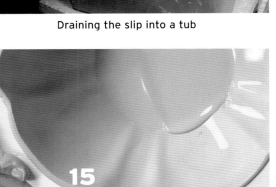

15

Spreading residual slip across the floor of the casting

Richard Shaw

Still Life with Apples and Palette, 2005
8 ½ x 22 x 9 ½ inches (21.6 x 55.9 x 24.1 cm)
Slip-cast porcelain; glaze, cone 6; engobe, pencil; underglaze
Photo by Charles Kennard

135

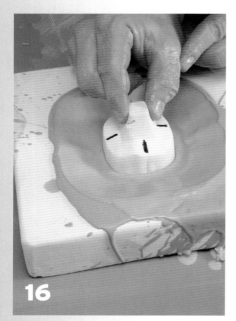

16

Placing the dusted footwell mold into the saucer casting

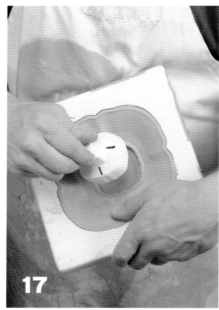

17

Removing the footwell mold from the casting

18

Emptying a mold with a drain tube

If you're casting a saucer, this is the point at which you should create the footwell. Dust the footwell form with Chinese dust (see page 139) and press it firmly into the center of the saucer, displacing some of the residual slip that has settled on the saucer floor (see photo 16). When the slip around the footwell form has dried, remove the form. In its place, you'll see a beautiful recess in which the cup will rest (see photo 17).

Some small molds—for lids, tumblers, spouts, and feet, for example—can be set in an inverted or perpendicular position after draining. Because not much residual slip is left in these molds, no lines will develop in the castings if the molds are inverted to dry. (This is another reason I prefer very liquid slip: it makes the draining process as quick and efficient as possible.)

While the mold is casting or just after you drain it, you may notice a sharp, clean line on the inside top edge of the casting. If the mold has been fed new slip during the casting, the level of the added slip often creates another fine line. But when you pour the slip out of the mold, these lines are covered up. This was one of the first things I noticed when I began casting. The line was a wonderful detail that I wanted to preserve, but every method I tried for removing the slip from the mold disturbed it. Eventually I came up with an effective technique. Using a wet/dry shop vacuum with a crevice tool removed the slip from the mold quickly but left the line intact. This slip line can't be formed in any other way and is incredibly beautiful.

draining molds with drain tubes

When draining molds with drain tubes, unscrew the caps and let them drain (see photo 18). A mold of this type will usually have to be tilted and propped up so that all the residual slip on its floor flows toward the drain tube. Make sure your bucket is large enough to collect all the slip. Slip running out of a mold, into a bucket, and onto the floor is always an unwelcome sight! Remember to patch the hole in the casting with a small scrap of casting slip that hasn't dried yet and is still malleable (see photo 19).

19

Patching the drain-tube hole in the casting

Draining a mold with one small opening can be difficult because the slip can seal the hole closed, and an opening that isn't large enough won't allow air in as the slip drains out. I encountered this difficulty while draining a double-gourd vase mold. The slip drained out easily, but as it came through the waist of the form, it created a vacuum inside the casting, which caused the soft casting to collapse inside the mold.

The solution is to introduce a small stream of compressed air into the mold. The air displaces the slip, the slight pressure keeps the casting from collapsing, and the pressurized air also helps push the slip out of the mold very quickly. Before draining the mold, I fit a straight plastic drinking straw onto a compressor blowgun and adjust the regulator to yield barely a puff of air. (I test the adjustment by putting the tip of the blowgun in my mouth and turning up the regulator until it takes about two seconds to fill my cheeks. This sounds inelegant, but it works.) I place the straw on the blowgun, turn the mold onto its side, insert the straw into the mold, and pull the trigger on the blowgun until the slip begins to flow out. Then I invert the mold so the slip drains into the neck and out of the mold. Blowguns can be purchased with a variety of attachments, including a long tube that's perfect for draining these types of molds.

REMOVING CASTINGS FROM MOLDS

As the casting rests in the mold, it's dried by both the air and the plaster mold. Remove the overpour from the rim of the mold with a fettling knife (see photo 20). In time the casting will naturally shrink away from the mold walls. With most simple molds, this process takes 15 to 30 minutes.

20

Cutting the overpour off the rim of a mold

To remove a casting from a light one-piece mold, place a board over the top of the mold, flip the mold and board over in midair, and set them on the work surface. With larger molds, hold the board tightly on top of the mold, lift one edge, and roll the mold over without picking it up. Lift the mold off the casting. If you want the form to be upright, place a second board on the bottom of the form and flip it back over between the two boards (see photo 21). As you'll quickly discover, the weight of the mold will determine the method you use.

21

Flipping the casting from one board to another

Chris Gustin

Alcobaca Vase #2023, **2000**
27 x 8 x 8½ inches (68.6 x 20.3 x 21.6 cm)
Slip-cast porcelain; wood fired in anagama kiln, cone 11
Photo by Dean Powell

Linda Cordell

Pink Blush, 2004
12 x 18 x 10 inches (30.5 x 45.7 x 25.4 cm)
Modeled and cast, china clay slip; cone 10, reduction
Photo by artist

22

Lifting a casting out of its mold

Small forms such as tumblers and small lidded forms can be lifted out of the molds without much deformation (see photo 22). Two-piece molds are split open, like shells, to remove the castings. Multiple-piece molds are disassembled in sequence, and the casting is then removed. I try to remove the casting as soon as the pot will stand on its own. Experience will teach you the right timing.

releasing castings from complex molds

With more complicated forms and those with undulating curves, castings should be released from the mold before they release of their own accord. Loosening the casting from the mold is essential; if it isn't loosened, it may not survive the drying process in the mold and may also be subject to cracking. While slip dries, it shrinks, sometimes in more than one direction at a time. Imagine pulling a piece of cloth very taut over the edge of a knife;

eventually the knife will cut the cloth. Similarly, a mold will stress and crack the casting.

The most useful way to eliminate this problem is by shooting compressed air between the mold and the casting in order to loosen the casting (see photo 23). A medium pressure is usually sufficient. While shooting the air, place one hand on the inside of the casting. Sometimes the air won't flow easily between the mold and casting; instead, it will form a bubble in the casting. If this happens, just press the casting back in place. (The casting will take a bit longer to stiffen up after this kind of deformation.) Once the casting is loose, allow it to continue drying in the mold until it will stand under its own weight without collapsing.

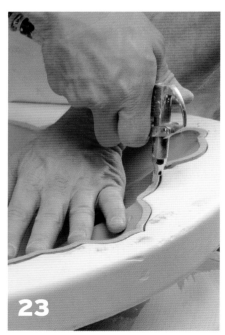

23

Loosening a casting from a mold with compressed air

25

Applying dirty water to a mold

26

Pressing the crack together after filling it with slip

24

Dusting the interior mold for a hollow-cast foot

dusting & dirty water

If you've experienced difficulties releasing castings from a particular mold, try this solution: Use a dusting sock to coat the mold interior generously with nepheline syenite or Chinese dust before you assemble the mold for casting. This coating—a very coarse field of nonplastic particles—on the casting surface prevents the slip from sticking to the mold.

An ancient Chinese alternative to nepheline syenite—and one that I prefer—is calcined clay. Classic Song dynasty bowls with carved decorations on their interiors were formed on bisque-fired clay hump molds. The decoration was carved in the mold and then transferred to the bowl. The Chinese solution to the problem of clay shrinking around the mold was to dust the hump mold lightly with the calcined powder of the same clay body before placing the slab over the mold. To finish the exterior details, the slab was then thrown on a wheel. The bisque-fired hump mold dried the paper-thin bowl very quickly, and the dusting of calcined clay allowed the bowl to release from the mold quite easily. In addition, because the dusting

powder was exactly the same as the clay body, there was no visible difference after the clay was fired. To make Chinese dust, dry-mix 500 grams of the casting slip and bisque fire it in a bowl. Use this mixture in a new gym sock to dust the molds.

Residual nepheline syenite, if left in the casting, will melt during firing and leave pockmarks in its surface. Sponging away all the marks that it leaves on the casting takes some time. Chinese dust, however, leaves marks on the cast surface but cleans up quite quickly.

On forms such as hollow-cast feet (see pages 88–89), using Chinese dust on the section of the mold that casts the inside of the foot is imperative (see photo 24). Because the slip will shrink around the plaster in this area, the plaster mold section must be removed from the casting before the casting cracks. Chinese dust makes this possible.

The outside and top of the foot, however, must stick to the mold as you remove the center. To make it stick, coat the mold with what's known as *dirty water*—water from the bucket that you use to sponge your finished pots (see photo 25). Mixed slip and water will also work. The fine particles of clay will embed themselves in the surface of the mold and hold the casting in place slightly longer than normal. Once you've removed the center, you can release the casting with compressed air to ensure that it doesn't crack.

HANDLING WET CASTINGS

Forms are very soft at this point and must be handled with care. Casting slip isn't plastic, but it is somewhat flexible in this soft state. Leaving the pots undisturbed as they transition to leather hard is best. I always check to see if cracks have developed in problem areas, so that I can fix them before the slip dries completely. Cracks that develop while the casting is drying in the mold or after removal are easy to repair. Add a small amount of water to 3 tablespoons (44 ml) of slip; it should be runnier, but not watery. Fill a brush with the diluted slip, open the crack, and brush in the slip to fill the crack completely. Push the two sides back together and let the casting dry (see photo 26).

Inevitably, you'll have some castings that haven't worked and that must be discarded. I used to throw bad castings into the scrap barrel to dry, and then mix them into new slip later. Over time my scrap volume grew to about 500 pounds (226.8 kg)—enough to fill a 30-gallon (113.6 L) trashcan.

When I generate a lot of castings that have to be recycled, I reduce the amount of scraps that I have to recycle by dipping the wasted castings in water while they're wet and throwing them back into the blunger at the end of the daily casting cycle. If you do this, check the specific gravity of the slip to make sure that the water-to-clay ratio is within the acceptable range.

Rebekah Bogard

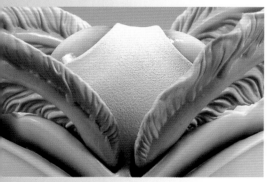

Media Nox, 2003
24 x 39 x 12 inches (61 x 99.1 x 30.5 cm)
Slip cast and press molded; underglaze, glaze;
electric fired, cone 04
Photo by artist

ASSEMBLING CAST PARTS

Before assembling cast forms, you must remove any excess clay formed by the pour holes on spouts and handles. Always use a very sharp knife, such as a craft knife, to make a clean cut in the stiffened casting slip. Cast clay tends to be nonplastic and will tear very easily if you use dull knives, such as most fettling knives.

One of the wonderful things about slip-cast ware is that when you assemble a form, all the parts have the same moisture content, so you don't have to score the attachment contact area! If you've scratched marks in the molds to indicate the registration of two parts, line them up before adding the attachment slip. Simply dip the attachment into casting slip, apply slip to it with a squeeze bottle, or paint some slip onto it with a brush, and, while the slip is still liquid, stick the attachment onto the form. The wet slip will dry within a few seconds of sticking the two parts together. Remove any excess slip with a brush dipped in water or a wet sponge. This attachment sequence is the same for spouts, handles, feet, knobs, and sprigs.

With small inset lids, such as the lid of my *Rock Teapot* (see page 105), a little trimming of both the lid and flange is often necessary to get them to fit. In the past I cut away the excess clay from the flange before fitting the lid to the body. In the process I flexed the flange area, which put stress on it. Radial cracks would then show up in the glaze firing. To avoid this problem, place the lid on the form to check the fit, then remove it and cut away the excess flange material. After cutting the flange, smooth the sharp edge; this eliminates cracking on inset lids. Place the lid back on the body for drying.

If your flanged lid is large and would be difficult to lift onto the form in its wet state, attach the handle and let the lid dry further as it sits on the flange mold. When the lid is stiff enough, lift it by the handle and place it on the body. Cap lids should be turned out onto a board to dry further and then set on the body.

To attach a handle, first dip it in casting slip (see photo 27). Then position it on the pot (see photo 28). Finally, sponge the excess slip from around the handle (see photo 29). Because a hollow-cast handle may expand during firing if it's completely sealed, make a pinhole in an inconspicuous place. Slip-cast handles that look like pulled handles often need to be modified when they're attached to cups (see photo 30).

When attaching feet, I usually invert the form first and then attach the foot (see photo 31). Sponge away the excess slip from inside and outside the foot (see photo 32). Some feet, however, are very large and will easily warp out of shape. Instead of adding the foot to the pot, I turn the foot out onto a board and leave it in an upright position. I squirt a bead of casting slip onto the foot's attachment area (see photo 33). Then I set the body of the form in place on the foot, aligning them very carefully (see photo 34). Clean off any extra slip with a brush or a sponge. To reduce the weight of feet for medium-sized forms, cut away the interior of the casting prior to attachment (see photo 35).

To attach spouts, first cut either one large hole or several small strainer holes in the body where you marked a location for the spout. (Liquid must be able to flow out of the pot.) Next, attach the spout by dipping its attachment

27

Dipping a handle in slip

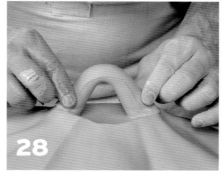

28

Attaching a handle to a lid

29

Cleaning up excess slip with a sponge

30

Adjusting the opening of a cup handle

31

Attaching a foot to its bowl

32

Sponging off excess slip

33

Applying slip to a hollow-cast foot

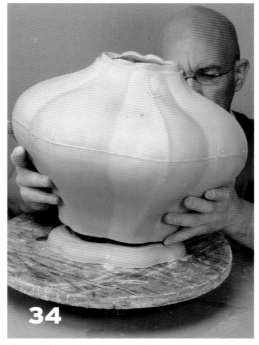

34

Placing the body onto the foot

35

Cutting away the interior of a cast foot

141

area in slip and placing it over the cut hole or holes, making sure that you align it correctly (see photo 36). Remove any excess slip. Then, using a craft knife with a long blade, cut open the tip of the spout and detail the spout as desired (see photo 37). Smooth the edges with a soft brush.

The rims of some forms must be cut down to give them the right look. Bowls, pitchers with irregular rims, and flanges are three such examples. Cutting just after casting works best (see photo 38).

Other than the exceptions I've noted in the preceding sections, I usually do minimal cleanup of edges and seams before drying, and in some cases, none at all. You can sponge the edges of bowls lightly, especially if any tearing occurred when you cut off the casting overpour (see photo 39). If you've cut a portion of the casting, such as the tip of a spout or the rim of a bowl, sponge the cut edges to soften them.

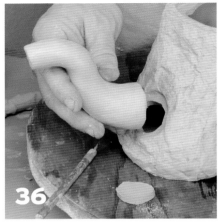

36

Attaching a spout to a teapot

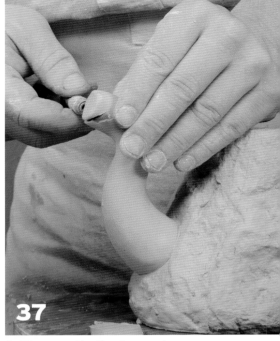

37

Cutting open the tip of a spout

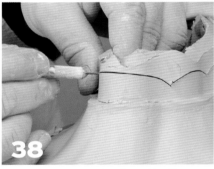

38

Removing excess clay from the flange of a jar

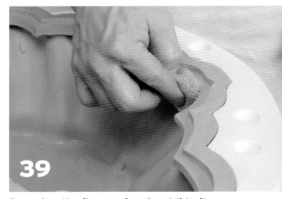

39

Sponging the flange of an inset lid after removing the excess clay

Rain Harris

Cherry Crush, 2005
44 feet x 19 inches (13.4 m x 48.3 cm)
Slip-cast stoneware; bisque, cone 1; mixed media
Photo by Doug Weisman

142

DRYING THE FINISHED CASTINGS

Most pieces can be left in the open to dry. Unlike thrown pottery, which is compressed and very plastic, and thus releases water slowly, water escapes from cast ware very quickly. As a precautionary measure, complex assembled forms are generally dried more slowly. The only consistent cracking problem I've experienced during drying is that thin handles tend to split apart if they're dried too quickly. Drying these forms slowly by covering them with plastic sheeting also allows you to repair any cracks that develop.

PREPARING THE DRIED CASTINGS FOR FIRING

Once the castings have dried, begin the final cleanup by gathering a bucket or tub of clean water, a sharp fettling knife, a craft knife, and several soft sponges. An important tip here: Slip-cast green ware is much more fragile than wheel-thrown pottery. Handle the cast pieces very gingerly. After a few pieces break, the right touch will become obvious!

Dip the edges of feet and rims in water. I dip two or three pieces at a time. Then scrape the edges to dull any sharp areas. They'll look rough, but don't worry. Use a sharp knife to scrape the seams on the side of the form, too. Scrape the seams on corners to match the corners' angles. On rounded forms, use a metal rib to scrape the seams so they meld with the curves.

After you've scraped all the seams and edges, smooth them with a very wet sponge. A sponge that's too dry will leave marks on the form. If you see any marks, go over them again. Slip parti-

cles loosen up when they're dampened. If you add enough water, the particles will float up into the water and then back down again, in a process similar to the sedimentation that happens during casting. As a result, they'll leave a very smooth surface. Throw any broken pots and scraps into a barrel for recycling into a new batch of casting slip.

preparing tile setters

Throughout the casting process, you should also cast a number of tile setters to use in the glaze fire (see page 71). You'll place these under forms that have feet or that have very fluid glazes. As soon as a setter is cast and removed from its mold, brush on a coating of kiln wash and allow it to dry with the clay. If the brush leaves ridges in the kiln wash, shave them down with a metal rib when they're bone dry. Then fire the green setters in the glaze kiln.

firing the castings

The bisque-firing process for slip-cast forms is the same as the bisque for thrown pieces, except that slip-cast clay can be fired much more quickly; casting slip isn't compressed and is nonplastic, so the particles release water easily. I usually warm up the kiln on medium for an hour and then turn it to high. This seemed risky at first, but it works fine. I bisque more slowly only when I'm firing large slip-cast pieces.

If you glaze fire in an electric kiln, use an alumina and kaolin kiln wash. Silica and kaolin kiln wash will attract sodium vapors from the glaze, and over time the kiln wash will begin to get glassy. When this occurs, pots will warp as they try to shrink because they stick to the glass on the kiln shelf. Even worse, they'll chip when you remove them.

Kohler Company refires sanitary ware in order to correct glaze flaws. After seeing how well this worked, I began to do it myself. Often the glaze doesn't flow enough, or it runs too much and needs grinding down and refiring in order to heal the grind mark. Or a spot will crawl, or a blister will develop in the glaze. In all these cases, refiring is an excellent solution. Sometimes pieces are refired to the original glaze temperature; in other cases, more flux is added to the glaze, and the pieces are fired several cones lower. I fire at cone 7 and refire at cone 3.

Pots should be warmed up to about 200°F (93.3°C) in the kiln before reglazing. Add more flux to the liquid glaze before firing. (I use Feno Frit 3110.) Also, to flocculate the glaze, add vinegar until it thickens. If a lot of refiring is required, mix a batch of glaze with less water. Apply the glaze with a brush to the areas that need it. The warm pot will dry the glaze as you apply it, so it won't run during the application.

CLEANING UP & STORING MOLDS

When the casting cycle is finished, the molds must be cleaned of any residual casting slip, then reassembled and stored. Use a rubber rib to remove any large sheets or chunks of slip, and sponge off the rest. Assemble the molds, band them together, and store them. If you have a drying cabinet, you can use it for mold storage. See page 19 for more information on cleaning and drying molds.

troubleshooting

Most technical problems are easily solved; others are creative challenges. I've noticed that the most difficult problems also lead to the most interesting technical breakthroughs.

REPAIRING A BROKEN MOLD

Sometimes a section of a mold that you've made is too thin for production, or perhaps the mold has broken. The procedure for repairing both conditions is the same. Plaster patches will hold broken pieces together and will also thicken molds that are too thin.

To create a patch, start by drilling holes in the exterior surfaces of all the mold sections, sizing them to correspond to the size of the mold (see photo 1). Holes in small molds should be smaller than holes in large molds. Drill these holes at angles so that they form undercuts. Be careful not to drill so deeply that the drill bit goes right through the plaster to the interior of the mold.

Next, soak the mold sections in water until they're fully saturated so the plaster won't absorb water from the patch. After the plaster is saturated, dry the plaster surfaces and be sure to clean any residual plaster or water out of the drilled holes. Reassemble the mold, holding the broken sections in place with blocking clay.

As you create the exterior patch, make sure you fill the drilled holes with plaster so the patch will be held securely in place (see photo 2). For most patching

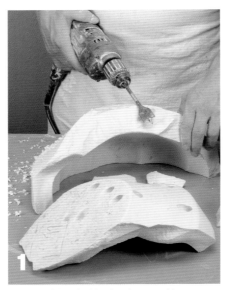
Holes drilled in the broken mold

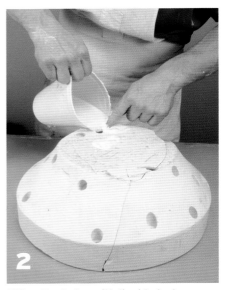
Filling the holes with liquid plaster

Frosting the patch on the broken mold

and repair jobs, you can simply frost the mold by hand (see photo 3). As the plaster enters the plastic stage, smooth it down with ribs. Then level the bottom (see photo 4).

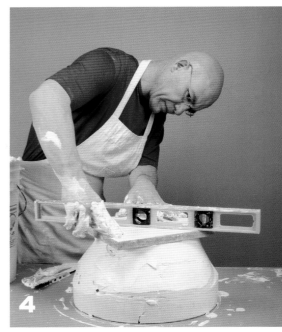
Leveling the bottom of the patched mold

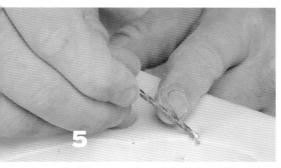

5

Drilling an undercut hole in a chipped mold

If, as you begin, the frosted patch looks as if it's drying up where it touches the broken mold, the mold isn't completely water-saturated or sealed well enough. Disassemble the mold immediately, wash it off, and repatch it after soaking it in water until it is saturated.

Now prepare the interior of the mold for patching. Because the exterior patch will have dried the mold somewhat, you must resoak the mold in water. Drill ¼-inch-deep (.6 cm) holes or carve undercuts with a craft knife. If the mold break was clean, you needn't fill the crack itself. The line left by the crack will leave a mark on the casting, but you can easily sponge this mark off. Frost the damaged areas with plaster, and smooth them with rubber ribs, leaving a little excess plaster that you can shave with a metal rib or sand away after the patch has cured.

REPAIRING A CHIPPED MOLD

Repairing chips on the edge of a mold or air bubbles on its surface is similar to repairing a broken mold. First, soak the mold in water. Drill small undercut holes around the chipped area. (Small chips may require only one or two holes). Then fill these holes with wet plaster (see photos 5 and 6). As the plaster sets, smooth it to the form of the mold (see photo 7). Don't scrape the wet plaster too much; leave any roughness to be sanded down after the plaster is set.

6

Filling the holes to patch the chipped area

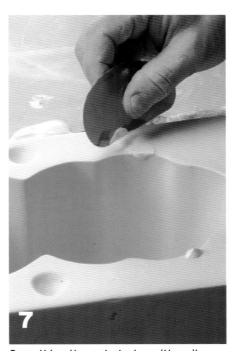

7

Smoothing the wet plaster with a rib

Denise Pelletier

Vapours (installation at Skulpturens Hus, Stockholm, Sweden), 2005
10 x 12 x 30 feet (3 x 3.7 x 9.1 meters)
Slip-cast and altered invalid feeders; vitreous china clay, oxidation, cone 10
Photo by artist
Work created in Arts/Industry, a program of the John Michael Kohler Arts Center

REMEDYING THE "PLASTER DISASTER"

While experimenting with mold making, you're likely to encounter what I call the "Plaster Disaster," which happens when a plaster-retaining system (assembled cottles, for example) fails and the liquid plaster spills everywhere. Initially, you may believe that your mold is in jeopardy, but you can remedy the situation if you act immediately.

Reassemble the retaining system first. Then you'll need to mix and pour more plaster before the first pour enters the heat cycle (approximately 10 to 12 minutes after pouring). If you were still pouring the plaster when it spilled, don't throw away the remaining liquid plaster; just scrape the plaster from the sides of the bucket and into the bottom. Leave the spilled plaster where it is and clean it up later so that you can act quickly to save the mold.

Calculate how much more plaster you'll need in order to make up the volume you want to fill. Measure the water and pour it into the residue from the first mix. Measure the plaster and quickly sift it through your fingers into the water. Because the residual plaster in the bucket will already have started to set, it will accelerate the setting time of the new plaster. Therefore, the normal mixing and setting schedule won't apply; you'll have to move quickly.

The first pour of plaster into the mold should still be in the plastic state, so make numerous deep indentations in it with your fingers (see photo 8). These undercuts will help the two mixtures lock together. Mix the new batch of plaster as soon as it is fully wetted, and when it is homogeneous, pour it on

8 Preparing for a second pour by making undercuts in the wet plaster

9 Completing the mold with a second pour of plaster

top of the first pour (see photo 9). Even when your cottles don't leak, you can use this same procedure to add additional plaster. If the first pour is already in the heat cycle, though, don't pour any more.

Jori Cheville Hebert

Untitled, 2005
32 x 32 x 5 inches (81.3 x 81.3 x 12.7 cm)
Slip cast, stoneware slip; skutt kiln, clear matte glaze; cone 5, acrylic paint, wood
Photo by Stephen Hebert

TROUBLESHOOTING PLASTER

Here is a guide to common technical difficulties and their solutions.

DRY PLASTER IS LUMPY

CAUSE Exposure to water (or there's a cat in the studio!)
CURE Sift out the lumps, or discard the plaster if it's old. Close the plaster bag tightly when it's not in use.

PLASTER SETS TOO QUICKLY

CAUSE The plaster is too old.
CURE Replace the old plaster with new.

CAUSE Dirty mixing equipment
CURE Clean all plaster residue off buckets and mixing blades.

PLASTER SECTIONS STICK TOGETHER

CAUSE Insufficient mold soap
CURE Apply more layers of soap next time, as well as spray mold release.

CAUSE Plaster was poured too soon, dissolving the mold soap
CURE Allow plaster setting to progress further before pouring

CAUSE Undercuts in the mold
CURE Use a pastry scraper and rubber mallet to force the mold apart, or redesign the mold.

CAUSE Overexpansion of mold sections during the setting cycle
CURE Wait for the mold to cool before disassembling it.

PLASTER TAKES TOO LONG TO SET

CAUSE Incorrect consistency (too much water or too little plaster)
CURE Mix another batch. Make sure to measure the plaster and water correctly, adding more plaster or less water as required.

PLASTER IS TOO SOFT

CAUSE Incorrect consistency (too much water or too little plaster)
CURE Mix another batch. Make sure to measure the water and weigh the plaster correctly, adding more plaster or less water as required.

CAUSE The plaster hasn't been mixed long enough.
CURE Mix longer.

CAUSE Molds were dried at a temperature greater than 125°F (51.7°C).
CURE Remake the mold; dry it with a fan at a lower temperature.

POOR FIT OF MOLD SECTIONS

CAUSE Mold sections were dried separately and warped during drying.
CURE Soak the molds in water, band them tightly together, and redry them.

PINHOLES IN MOLD SURFACE

CAUSE Small air bubbles remained trapped in the plaster because the plaster was mixed by hand.
CURE Mix the plaster with a drill and propeller; do not allow whirlpooling.

CAUSE Insufficient soaking
CURE Soak the plaster three to five minutes before mixing.

Paul McMullan

Rabbit, 2005
22 x 15 x 9 inches (55.9 x 38.1 x 22.9 cm)
Slip cast, slab built; underglaze, cone 04; oxidation glaze
Photo by Jerry Mathieson

10

Filling air bubbles with wet plaster

AIR BUBBLES IN CASTING SURFACE

CAUSE Plaster was splashed on the prototype during pouring.

CURE Remake the mold, pouring plaster down the wall of the retaining system, allowing it to flow up around the form; or soak the existing mold in water, fill the holes with plaster, and then sand the surface.

CAUSE Plaster started to set during frosting of the mold.

CURE Soak the mold in water, fill the holes with plaster, then sand the surface (see photo 10).

CAUSE Plaster was mixed by hand, and small air bubbles remained in it.

CURE Mix plaster with a drill and propeller; do not allow whirlpooling.

SLIP DOES NOT ABSORB IN CERTAIN AREAS

CAUSE Mold soap has not been removed from the casting surface.

CURE Sponge the area with white vinegar and then with water, or sand it with wet/dry sandpaper.

TROUBLESHOOTING SLIP & CASTING

SLIP GELS IN THE BUCKET

CAUSE Too much deflocculant

CURE Add another small batch of clay and water, with no deflocculant, or add a few drops of vinegar or 1 to 2 ounces (29.6 to 59.1 ml) of barium carbonate.

CAUSE The slip has too many plastic clays.

CURE Reduce the ball clay and increase the EPK; exchange the ball clay for a coarser-particle ball clay; or use clays with a lower exchange rate.

CAUSE The water is too hard.

CURE Use pond water, distilled water, rain water, or deionized water.

CASTING INTERIOR STAYS WET LONG AFTER MOLD HAS BEEN DRAINED

CAUSE The slip is too plastic and retains too much water.

CURE Reduce the ball clay and increase the EPK.

CAUSE The slip needs more deflocculant.

CURE Add more deflocculant.

Heather Mae Erickson

Whiteware, 2006
5 x 16 x 8 inches (12.7 x 40.6 x 20.3 cm)
Plaster models, porcelain slip; oxidation fired, cone 6
Photo by Ken Yanoviak

CASTING COLLAPSES IN THE MOLD

CAUSE During draining, a vacuum is created, pulling the casting from the mold.
CURE Drain the mold more slowly, or blow a slight stream of compressed air inside the casting during draining.

CAUSE The slip retains too much water.
CURE Reduce the ball clay and increase the EPK, or exchange the ball clay in the recipe for a coarser-particle ball clay.

CASTINGS CRACK WHILE DRYING OR WILL NOT RELEASE FROM THE MOLD

CAUSE Too much EPK or too little ball clay
CURE Reduce the EPK or increase the ball clay.

HOLES IN THE RIM OF AN INSET LID

CAUSE Air was trapped under the flange mold during casting.
CURE Scratch several lines from the top of the flange to the edge of the mold.

CASTING STICKS TO THE MOLD

CAUSE The mold is too wet.
CURE Dry the mold and cast it again.

CAUSE Too much EPK
CURE Reduce the EPK and increase the ball clay.

CASTING TEARS WHEN MOLD IS DISASSEMBLED

CAUSE The casting has not released from the mold.
CURE Wait longer and/or loosen the casting with compressed air.

CAUSE Not enough elasticity in the clay
CURE Replace some of the EPK with ball clay.

CASTINGS ARE SOFT & COLLAPSE AFTER REMOVAL FROM THE MOLD

CAUSE The slip is retaining too much water.
CURE Reduce the ball clay and increase the EPK.

CAUSE The castings are too wet to support their own weight.
CURE Allow the castings to dry longer in the mold.

PINHOLES IN THE CAST OR FIRED POT

CAUSE Small air bubbles in the casting slip
CURE Mix the slip longer, at a low speed.

CAUSE The slip is too thick and will not release fine air bubbles.
CURE Add more deflocculant to reduce the viscosity, and mix longer at low speed.

Chris Gustin

Alcobaba Vase #9940, 1999
22 x 8 x 8 inches (55.9 x 20.3 x 20.3 cm)
Slip-cast porcelain; wood fired in anagama kiln, cone 11
Photo by Dean Powell

about the author

about the author

Andrew Martin

Tamba Tums, 2000
5 ½ x 3 x 3 inches (13 x 7.6 x 7.6 cm)
Slip-cast porcelain; wood fired, cone 12
Photo by Nick Elias

Andrew Martin earned his B.F.A. from the Kansas City Art Institute in 1979 and his M.F.A. from Alfred University in 1984. He has had two residencies at the Archie Bray Foundation and has been a resident in the Arts-Industry Program at the Kohler Company. He has been awarded two Fellowship Grants from the National Endowment for the Arts and has worked in the Reproduction Department at the Metropolitan Museum of Art.

While at Alfred, Andrew visited Greece and Turkey. In the Minoan pots of Crete and the Isnik tiles of Instanbul, he found visual links through historical ceramics that gave voice to his seminal intuitions about form, glaze color, decoration, beauty, and use. His pots are noted for their fluidity, volume, and structure; his innovative forming is the subject of this book.

Andrew operated Martin Porcelain in Denver, Colorado, for seven years and produced more than 18,000 pots during that time. He has taught dozens of workshops across the United States and Canada, has exhibited nationally and internationally, and has written essays and articles for *American Ceramics* and *Ceramics Monthly*. He has been a moderator and presenter at the annual conference of the National Council on Education in the Ceramic Arts (NCECA) and at the Utilitarian Clay: Celebrate the Object conference at Arrowmont School of Crafts. In addition, Andrew has taught at the University of Colorado, Alfred University, the University of Denver, and Dominican University.

appendixes

APPENDIX A: plaster-mixing ratios

The chart below lists the amounts of water and dry plaster required for commonly mixed volumes of plaster. The consistencies are calculated using a ratio of 66 (29.9 kg) pounds of water to 100 pounds (45.4 kg) of plaster.

Water		Plaster		Total Volume	
Quarts (liters)		Pounds (kilograms)		Cubic inches (liters)	
0.5	(0.47)	1.5	(0.68)	40	(0.66)
1	(0.95)	3	(1.4)	80	(1.3)
2	(1.9)	6	(2.7)	160	(2.6)
3	(2.9)	9	(4.1)	240	(3.9)
4	(3.8)	12	(5.4)	320	(5.2)
5	(4.8)	15	(6.8)	400	(6.6)
6	(5.7)	18	(8.2)	480	(7.8)
7	(6.6)	21	(9.5)	560	(9.2)
8	(7.6)	24	(10.9)	640	(10.5)
9	(8.5)	27	(12.3)	720	(11.8)
10	(9.5)	30	(13.6)	800	(13.1)

APPENDIX B: casting-slip recipes

Kohler Cone 10 Slip

This slip is used to cast sanitary ware at Kohler Co. Because the ware is handled by many people and glazed in the green-ware state, this slip has a high ball-clay content to give the green ware additional strength.

Materials	%
FC Kaolin	12
C & C Ball Clay	16
L-1 Ball Clay	25
Black Charm Ball Clay	5
Bandy Black Ball Clay	2
NC-4 Feldspar	18
Flint	22
TOTAL	100
Water	40
Sodium Silicate	0.25–0.5

Mackenzie-Childs Cone 04 Terra-Cotta Slip

Although this slip defies all assumptions about casting slip, it works very well. It consists of three parts clay to one part nonplastics. (Note that the total is 105 parts, rather than 100 parts.)

Materials	%
Ball Clay	4.8
Redart	47.6
Goldart	23.9
Talc	4.8
Flint	9.5
Frit 3110	9.5
TOTAL	100.0
Water	40
Darvan	0.4–0.6

Martin Cone 10 Porcelain Slip

Its high ball-clay content makes this slip very accommodating for elaborate forms. It is slightly gray when fired in reduction but acceptably white in oxidation.

Materials	%
Grolleg Kaolin	3
EPK Kaolin	6
Spinks Blend Ball Clay	7
SGP Ball Clay	7
Custer	25
Flint	25
TOTAL	100
Water	40
Sodium Silicate	0.25

Spleth Cone 10 Slip

This slip is whiter and more translucent than most casting bodies because its ball-clay content is relatively low. It is somewhat less plastic than the Martin Cone 10 Porcelain Slip provided above.

Materials	%
Grolleg Kaolin	35
EPK Kaolin	7
SGP Ball Clay	8
Pyrotrol	7
Custer	18
Flint	25
TOTAL	100
Water	40
Sodium Silicate	0.25–0.5

Hensley/Polseno Cone 7 Slip

This is a very reliable and translucent body, and the ball clay content makes it good for casting elaborate forms. Try SGP ball clay, which tends to be a coarser-particle clay and which casts more quickly than OM-4 ball clay.

Materials	%
OM-4 Ball Clay	25
EPK Kaolin	18
Tile Clay #6 Kaolin	5
Nepheline Syenite	35
Custer	9
Frit 3110	1
Flint	7
TOTAL	100
Water	42
Sodium Silicate	0.25–0.5

glossary

Vladimir Groh & Yasuyo Nishida

Cup, 2006
4 x 4 inches (10.2 x 10.2 cm)
Slip-cast porcelain; shellac; gas fired,
2408 °F (1320 °C), patina overglaze
Photo by Vladimir Groh

alumina. Refractory material used in casting slip as a filler in addition to flint. Alumina also raises the firing temperature of the clay, imparting a high degree of fired strength, as in hotel china. In high percentages, it imparts opacity to both clay and glaze.

ball clay. The main constituent clay in some midrange and all low-fire casting bodies. Coarse-particle ball clays are used in slip because they release water more readily than fine-particle ball clays. Ball clays make slip plastic; they also make porcelain bodies less translucent due to their high levels of titanium.

banding wheel. A turntable for pottery.

bisque firing. A slow, low-temperature firing that hardens clay and leaves it porous, ready for glazing.

bloating. A process that occurs when a clay body is overfired. Results in lumps on the surface of the fired clay.

blocking. The process of using plastic clay to protect one portion of a form from plaster that will be poured onto another section.

blocking clay. Consists of white earthenware, made with 50 percent ball clay and 50 percent talc. Often used because it is very smooth. Used to make clay prototypes. *See also* **blocking and modeling clay.**

blunger. A motorized stationary shaft-and-propeller mixer used to mix casting slip in a tank. Commonly used in the pottery industry.

bone dry. The state of clay that has been completely air-dried but has not yet been fired.

calcine. To heat to a high temperature, but below the melting or fusing point.

casting. An object reproduced in clay by pouring casting slip into a mold. *See also* **slip casting.**

casting rate. The amount of time a casting slip remains liquid before it begins to gel.

casting slip. A deflocculated clay body formulated for slip casting and generally consisting of 50 percent clay and 50 percent nonplastics. Mixed with 40 parts water to 100 parts clay, and an added deflocculant.

CEC (Cation Exchange Capacity). The capacity of a clay to absorb cations (positively charged ions) on its surface. The higher the CEC of a clay, the more difficult it is to deflocculate.

chinese dust. A powdered, calcined dust made by bisque firing the dry ingredients of a casting slip. Used to help release a casting from the mold more easily in order to prevent cracking.

consistency. A number denoting the parts, by weight, of water to which 100 parts of plaster should be added in order to attain the correct absorption rate. For a consistency of 66, for example, 100 parts of plaster by weight are added to 66 parts of water by weight.

cottles. Boards that are clamped together in order to contain liquid plaster.

crazing. A condition that occurs when a glaze fits too tightly to the clay, causing small or large cracks in the glaze.

deflocculant. A soluble alkali that keeps clay particles suspended in clay slip.

deflocculation. The addition of deflocculants to slip, which changes the electrical charges on the edges of the clay particles from positive to negative, thus causing the particles to repel each other. With just enough water around each particle to create a small envelope, the particles float in the slip.

dirty water. Water with a bit of casting slip in it; sometimes water from the bucket used to sponge finished pots. When applied to the casting surface of a mold, dirty water leaves a deposit of very fine particles in the mold's pores; these hold the casting to the mold when it might otherwise peel loose.

dummy. A mock-up of a form, used to visualize the form's proportion. Not usually intended for actual casting.

dunting. A condition that occurs in fired wares, caused by insufficient flux in the clay. Results in the clay not being fused; literally tears the pot apart when the silica contracts at the quartz inversion stage in a firing.

dusting. Coating the casting surface of a mold with a substance that will prevent the casting from sticking, while still allowing the mold to absorb water.

Use talc for low-fire and nepheline syenite for high-fire. Bisque-fired casting slip (or Chinese dust) can be substituted in either low- or high-fire.

exchange rate. A number provided by clay suppliers that indicates how easily a clay will deflocculate. The lower the number, the more easily the clay will deflocculate. *See* **CEC (Cation Exchange Capacity).**

feldspar. A flux in clay bodies and a main constituent of many glazes.

fettle. The seam left on a casting, located where two mold sections meet.

fettling knife. A knife used to trim pour-hole waste and to remove fettles from cast green ware.

flange. The portion of a casting that ensures registration of the body and lid. May be on either the body or lid.

flint. Also known as silica, a material used in clay as a filler. Forms glass both in clay and in glaze.

flocculation. The forming of lumps or masses. In clay, the tendency of particles to attract each other due to the negative and positive charges on

their surfaces. The opposite of deflocculation.

flux. A material that melts the silica in a clay body or glaze.

footprint. The shape of the portion of a pot that sits on the table.

frit. A manufactured glaze, containing toxic or soluble materials, that is melted into glass, then ground into powder and used like feldspar or flux in glaze and sometimes in clay, in small amounts.

frosting. A method of applying viscous plaster or rubber to a form, as if frosting a cake.

gel. *See* **Thixotropic.**

green ware. Clay that has been completely dried and is ready for firing.

hydrometer. An instrument used to check the specific gravity of a liquid.

kaolin. The primary clay in porcelain bodies.

keys. Male and female fittings in a mold that make two or more pieces of the mold register together exactly.

David Pier

Coffee Cup Set, 2005
4 x 4 x 4¹/₂ inches (10.2 x 10.2 x 11.4 cm)
Slip cast from mold, porcelain slip; electric fired, cone 10, oxidation
Photo by artist

Anne Kraus

Lilac Vase, 1988
12 ½ x 9 inches (31.8 x 22.9 cm)
Slip cast
Photo by Tony Cunha
Courtesy of Garth Clark Gallery

kiln wash. Substance used to coat kiln shelves and setters in order to reduce sticking if glazes run. With cast ware, use 50 percent kaolin and 50 percent hydrated alumina.

leather hard. The stage at which clay is partly dry and stiff.

master mold. A positive form, made of plaster or rubber, usually cast from a mold and used to produce working molds. Also used to cast sculptures in cement, plaster, or wax. Rubber masters accommodate undercuts, such as those in handles.

model (n). The original form from which a mold is made; often referred to as the prototype.

model (v). To sculpt a form in clay.

modeling clay. Sold as white earthenware by ceramic suppliers. Consists of 50 percent ball clay and 50 percent talc. *See also* **blocking clay.**

mold soap. A sealant used to prevent a new pour of plaster from adhering to a previous pour.

mother mold. Plaster mold that supports a rubber master mold.

nepheline syenite. A naturally occurring mineral composed of feldspar and nephelite.

particle size. The microscopic measurement of clay particles, expressed in microns.

pitch. The degree of a steep downward curve

plastic clay. *See* **blocking clay; modeling clay.**

plastilene. An oil-based clay good for making prototypes of handles and spouts. Comes in a variety of working qualities, from very soft to very stiff.

porcelain. A white, high-fire, translucent clay body.

primary clays. Clays that are mined close to their origins and that therefore contain fewer contaminants than do secondary clays.

profile. The side view of a form.

prototype. The original form from which a mold is cast.

pyrophyllite. An alumina silicate with no fluxes and no plasticity, roughly analogous to calcined kaolin. Used as a filler in porcelain bodies and generally assumed to add strength to them, although this assumption has not proved to be true. More expensive than flint when used as a filler.

refractory. Resistant to melting or heat. The most refractory substances used in casting slips are alumina and silica; the least refractory are fluxes, such as feldspars and frits.

secondary clays. Clays that have been transported away from their original sources by natural forces such as erosion and glaciers, and that often pick up other materials during the process.

shape. The top view of a form.

silica, chemically combined. Silica introduced to the clay recipe in the form of clay. Silica and alumina are the two main constituents of clay.

silica, free. Silica added to the clay as ground quartz or flint.

slip. A liquid mixture of clay used for decoration or assembly of parts. Not necessarily casting slip; it may not be deflocculated. *See also* **casting slip.**

slip casting. A technique in which a suspension (slip) is poured into a porous mold, usually made of plaster.

slumping. The deformation of a pot during firing. Can occur with cast forms that tend to be somewhat flat or that have long, straight sides.

soda ash. Sodium carbonate. Used as a secondary deflocculant along with sodium silicate. Tends to make the casting slip retain more water and the casting more plastic.

sodium silicate. Used as a deflocculant; also known as "water glass."

specific gravity. The specific gravity of a material is the ratio of its density to the density of water weighed at a standard temperature and pressure. The specific gravity of water is 1 (100 cc of water weighs 100 grams). 100 cc of casting slip should weigh between 165 and 180 grams; thus, the specific gravity is expressed as 1.65 and 1.80.

spit out. Occurs when calcium in fired clay expands, breaking through the clay and leaving a pit in the clay surface.

Surform tools. A family of tools made by Stanley; useful for shaving plaster.

talc. A fine-grained mineral used as a flux in low-fire bodies.

template. A metal, plastic, or hardboard sheet on which clay is modeled to create a prototype.

terra sigillata. A smooth, lustrous coating of deflocuulated clay that resembles a glaze.

thixotropic. A property of casting slip, plastic clay, and plaster. In plaster, a stage at which the consistency is gel-like when at rest but fluid when agitated.

tile setter. A cast clay tile, coated with kiln wash, on which a form is fired in order to eliminate warping. Acts as a kind of sled, so that the piece being fired doesn't drag on the kiln shelf as the piece shrinks in the firing.

undercut. An undulation or indentation in a form that makes a multiple-piece mold necessary.

vent. A tube or scratch in a mold that vents air that would otherwise be trapped in the mold as it is filled with slip. Air is often trapped under the flange of an inset lid.

viscosimeter. An instrument that measures viscosity.

viscosity. The thickness or resistance to flow of a liquid.

vitrification. The melting (or maturing) of a clay or glaze caused by the heat of the firing. Fluxes act on the silica, melting the two together to the point at which the clay is dense, or nonabsorbent, and the glaze has formed glass.

waste mold. A mold that is used in an intermediate molding process and is eventually thrown away.

wedging board. A plaster surface on which plastic clay is kneaded in order to remove air and evenly redistribute moisture.

wet/dry sandpaper. Silicon carbide sandpaper, useful for sanding plaster. Comes in grades from 50-grit (coarse) to 600-grit (super fine).

working mold. A mold used for production, made either from a prototype or from a master mold.

Bruce Gholson

Emerald Fossil Fish, 2006
11 x 11 x 2 ¾ inches (27.9 x 27.9 x 7 cm)
Slip-cast porcelain; multiple molybdenum and crystalline glazes; electric fired, cone 8
Photo by Bulldog Pottery

contributing artists

Lauren Adams
Brooklyn, New York, page 9

David Alban
Monroe, New York, pages 30 and 111

Lesley Baker
Oakland, California, pages 60, 68, and 105

Rebekah Bogard
Reno, Nevada, page 140

Ginny Conrow
Seattle, Washington, page 123

Linda Cordell
Philadelphia, Pennsylvania, pages 66, 102, and 138

Craig Clifford
Long Beach, California, page 22

Larry J. Donahue
Wilmington, Delaware, page 14

Sanam Emami
Alfred, New York, page 52

Heather Mae Erickson
Thorofare, New Jersey, pages 11, 98 and 148

Paul Eshelman
Elizabeth, Illinois, pages 86 and 97

Ilena Finocchi
North Lima, Ohio, pages 70 and 95

Bruce Gholson
Seagrove, North Carolina, pages 18 and 155

Vladimir Groh
Brno, Czech Republic, pages 36, 65, 134, and 152

Chris Gustin
South Dartmouth, Massachusetts, pages 13, 53, 120, 137, and 149

Rain Harris
Columbus, Ohio, pages 24, 48, and 142

Rebecca Harvey
Columbus, Ohio, pages 38 and 117

Wes Harvey
Lubbock, Texas, pages 15, 44, and 132

Jori Cheville Hebert
Olathe, Kansas, page 146

Richard Hensley
Floyd, Virginia, pages 114, 115, and 159

Anne Kraus
New York, New York, pages 33, 34, 35, and 154

Sue Kay Lee
Las Vegas, Nevada, page 122

Amy Lenharth
Kansas City, Missouri, page 67

Andrew Martin
Los Angeles, CA, pages 3, 4, 6, 7, 38, 40, 43, 49, 50, 53, 54, 70, 76, 81, 87, 90, 92, 96, 100, 105, and 150

Mathew S. McConnell
Boulder, Colorado, pages 61, 119, and 158

Paul McMullan
Ann Arbor, Michigan, pages 19, 74, and 147

Ron Nagle
San Francisco, California, pages 21, 99, and 107

Charles B. Nalle
Melbourne Beach, Florida, pages 27 and 121

Yasuyo Nishida
Brno, Czech Republic, pages 36, 65, 134 and 152

Richard Notkin
Helena, Montana, pages 127 and 128

Dawn Oakford
Lenah Valley, Tasmania, Australia, page 78

Casey O'Connor
Rocklin, California, page 77

Denise Pelletier
Providence, Rhode Island, pages 87, 91, and 145

David Pier
Palo Alto, California, pages 10, 133, and 153

Donna Polseno
Floyd, Virginia, pages 112 and 113

Jesse Ross
Lincoln, Nebraska, pages 89 and 104

Judith Salomon
Shaker Heights, Ohio, pages 17 and 85

Amy Santoferraro
Akron, Ohio, pages 20, 84 and, 124

Richard Shaw
Fairfax, California, pages 43, 63, 71, 92, 103, and 135

Paula Smith
Rock Hill, South Carolina, page 118

Tom Spleth
Penland, North Carolina, pages 55, 56, and 57

Richard Swanson
Helena, Montana, pages 69 and 101

Steven Thurston
Bexley, Ohio, page 47

Lea Tyler
Warren, Vermont, pages 32 and 125

Von Venhuizen
Lubbock, Texas, page 72

Wendy Walgate
Ontario, Canada, pages 16 and 80

Simon Ward
Scotland, United Kingdom, pages 83 and 110

Maryann Webster
Salt Lake City, Utah, page 28

Julie York
Philadelphia, Pennsylvania, page 109

acknowledgments

This book would never have happened without five people: Suzanne Tourtillott, Nick Elias, Chris Rich, Megan Kirby, and Shannon Quinn-Tucker.

In the spring of 2006, Suzanne and I discussed the possibility of Lark Books revising and publishing my self-published book on mold making. Just a few months later, *The Essential Guide to Mold Making and Slip Casting* was finished. Suzanne shepherded this project through a very short production schedule and did so with remarkable ease and humor.

My longtime friend and photographer, Nick Elias, brought his great and uncompromising eye to the photography. He persisted through many long days of shooting and many long nights of postproduction adjustments to ensure that the images were perfect. Nick's participation in this project guaranteed that the images would be instructive and beautiful and have a distinct visual impact.

Chris Rich gave my text organization and polish beyond what I could have imagined. I marveled at her ability to understand the nuances of the process and to bring to light small details that helped to elaborate the descriptions. I could not have been more pleased with our working relationship and the results of her skill as an editor.

I appreciate everything that Shannon Quinn-Tucker did to help bring this book together. She did a superb job contacting the contributing artists and organizing their images, and she also provided critical backup to everyone involved.

Megan Kirby amassed everyone's efforts to present you with the beautiful book in your hands. With her skills and keen eye, Megan matched the high standards of the content, editing, and photography and made them all sing together.

My thanks also go to the artists whom I interviewed: Tom Spleth, Richard Notkin, Anne Kraus, Donna Polseno, and Richard Hensley. Their talents are inspirations to aspiring artists, and especially to those who choose to make their art with molds. Anne passed away in 2003. Anyone who values excellent work and an open heart will miss her as a person and as an artist. I do.

In addition, I am especially grateful to two close friends, Kathy Holt and Pete Pinnell, who helped clarify the technical and ceramic terminology. Sometimes Pete had to make the terminology clear to me first!

My previous version of this book would never have existed without the help of two very close friends: Melinda Israel and Craig Rouse. Melinda guided that book from conception to publication. She edited the text and gave it warmth and accessibility, and did both with astounding creative energy and insight. Craig, co-owner of ArtHouse Design in Denver, Colorado, contributed his expertise, artistry, and creativity. His visual standards, steadiness, and persistence were demonstrations of who he is as a person and as a designer.

Finally, to my parents, Howard and Jane Martin, both now deceased, I extend my love, appreciation, and thanks for the support and encouragement that you both gave me over the years. Your moral and ethical examples were demonstrated through your love, steadiness, persistence, loyalty, and humor. To Jane: You championed my being an artist; you obviously saw that art focused my life and passions in a positive direction. To Howard: I grew to feel your demonstrations in life and in our relationship as a positive legacy passed on from father to son and from man to man. I love you both.

index

Mathew S. McConnell

EASX05OK0805B13, 2005
13 x 14 x 7 inches (33 x 35.6 x 17.8 cm)
Slip-cast and assembled earthenware; cone 05
Photo by artist

Richard Hensley

Cast Teapot, 2006
6 x 9 x 4 inches (15.2 x 22.9 x 10.2 cm)
Assembled cast porcelain, pulled handle;
cone 10, reduction
Photo by Molly Morikawa